I0521151

THE GOSPEL OF ELYALITH

Published by Saklas Publishing

Olympia, Washington

ISBN: 979-8-9943016-6-1

This volume is presented as part of an ongoing archival reconstruction project. While inspired by historical frameworks, it remains a work of fiction. Names, characters, institutions, locations, and events are either products of the author's imagination or are used fictitiously. Any resemblance to actual persons, living or dead, or actual events is coincidental.

A∴A∴

Printed in the United States of America   1 3 5 7 9   10 8 6 4 2

AUTHOR'S NOTE

Any resemblance between the characters, figures, deities, angels, demons, archons, vanished priesthoods, submerged cosmologies, or half-forgotten gods appearing in these pages and any beings—real, historical, mythological, or currently worshiped—is purely coincidental. If something here seems familiar, that is a matter between the reader and their memory.

This is a work of "friction."

- There are writings within the tradition that speak of the Work vanishing for years, only to return in a single instant with greater force than before. –

- They also speak of the magician who performs countless meaningless calculations until one pattern suddenly reveals itself, as if it had been waiting behind all the rest. This is the nature of the Path: long silence, then a moment that explains everything.-

"Magick is the Science and Art of causing Change to occur in conformity with Will."
Crowley, A. (1997). Magick: Liber ABA, Book Four, Parts I–IV (H. B. Motta, Ed.). Weiser Books. (Original work published 1913)

THE REQUIREMENTS OF A

MAGICAL JOURNAL

A magical journal is a place where one tells the truth. Not doctrine, not interpretation, and not theory—only the record of what occurred.

The customs surrounding such a journal are simple.

Write precisely.
What was seen, felt, thought, or heard must be entered without adornment.

Write consistently.
A period of Work asks for continuity, so that nothing essential is lost between moments.

Write without embellishment.
Visions may speak in symbols; the record must remain faithful to the experience as it arrived.

Record the conditions.
The hour. The weather. The astrological sign or influence under which the entry was made. The state of mind. The state of body. The act performed. These details often reveal patterns the entry alone cannot show.

Date the Work as the Work requires.
The journal follows the current of the Work itself, not the conventions of the Julian calendar. The dating reflects the inner progression, not the outer almanac. Record the result with the same honesty as the quiet days. Breakthrough and silence stand on equal footing.

Aid in further initiations.
Write in such a manner that the Record may be fit to support further initiation; the discipline of its keeping must rise to the level required for advancement.

These modest principles governed the writing of this record. They are included here not to guide the reader, but to acknowledge the discipline under which the following pages were written.

RECORD OF THE TASK ASSIGNED TO FRATER LACHESIS PEYTON, 0°=0° Anno 120, Sun at 19 degrees Aries

Under the care of Frater K.

I, Frater Lachesis Peyton, 0°=0°, place this statement at the threshold of the Work contained in this book.

I was charged with the following instructions:

- Keep a magical journal, steady, truthful, and suitable for review.

- Select a chapter of Liber LXV for dedicated practice.

- Commit that chapter for perfect internal memory.

Nothing more was said.

I was given no curriculum, no commentary, no obvious key to the system. I was simply pointed toward the basic instructions, and told to bring with me *The Holy Books of Thelema.*

The responsibility to interpret the instruction—and to endure it—was entirely my own. By my own choosing, I selected Chapter III of *Liber LXV* and undertook the practice. For nine years, I held the chapter within me: the daily silent recitation, the correction of every lapse, the slow welding of text and consciousness until the chapter existed internally as something whole and unbroken.

When the Work was complete—not announced, not signified, but complete in itself—the moment arrived without ritual or warning.

It felt as though a hand pressed between my shoulders, and I was pushed into the pool.

There was no ceremony. No instruction to proceed. Only the sudden, irrevocable lightning-flash of understanding—the Vision that had waited behind nine years of silence.

What follows in this volume is the record of that single event. It is not analysis. It is not commentary. It is the Vision itself, written faithfully according to the discipline I was given. Every word, symbol, and sequence in the pages ahead is part of that record.

Frater Lachesis Peyton, 0°=0°
With humble respect to Frater K.

The Vision came, and so did the Voice—inseparable, immediate, transmitted beyond any quantifiable span. These are the words as they arrived.

This is what She told me—in silence.

GOSPEL of ELYALITH

THE GOSPEL OF ELYALITH

Written Under Custody, 2038 — Rev. Elias Markham

They keep me three levels below ground, in a room that does not officially exist. The lights never fully go out. The cameras are hidden badly enough that I know they want me to see them. The door has no handle on my side. Twice a day someone in a white coat comes in to take blood, and twice a day someone in a collar comes in to take notes. They do not yet know which of us is the more superstitious. I am told it is the year 2038.

On the last day I remember before the widening, it was 1940. There was a table, a crucifix, two examiners, a recorder wheel turning, and a sigil on old vellum that looked at me harder than any man in that room. There was a question I could not answer. There was a voice that was not mine speaking through my mouth. There was a sentence—the seal is breaking—and then there was no more room, no more walls, no more time in the shape I had known it.

From their point of view, I vanished in that instant. For them, nearly a century passed. For me, what happened in between is the reason this book exists. The men upstairs call what I lived through a "non-local event." They have transcripts and neurological reports and a label—Incident 12-Q—to keep it filed where it cannot contaminate their theology. They believed, for a while, that locking the papers away in a box and burying the box under Rome would be enough.

That box is Vault 77-A. It was not opened for my sake. It was opened because I walked into an English consulate in Dubai two months ago looking exactly as I did the night I disappeared, carrying none of the intervening years on my face, and told a bewildered young officer behind a reinforced glass screen: *"My name is Elias Markham. You have some of my things in Rome. I would like them back."*

They confirmed my identity with fingerprints taken in 1939 and with a recording of my voice from the interrogation tape the Church pretends it never made. They noticed that my collar was cut in a pattern that went out of use long before most of the consulate staff were born. They called their superiors. Their superiors called Rome. Rome did what Rome always does:

it pretended this was an emergency it had already foreseen. Within forty-eight hours I was back under the same authority that had lost me.

Now I sit in this cell while a different priest with a different title pores over the same fragments I once tried to send up the chain: abbey letters, Ardinus and Hadrian, the Goodcrow ledger, the sailor's unsent report, Lucas Meretti's hidden account, the NASA anomaly, the Facility Q transcript. They call the whole body of it the *Elyalith Dossier* now, as if giving it a name makes it theirs. It does not. They are re-evaluating Vault 77-A at this very moment. They think they are doing it to understand what I am. I am writing this to explain what they are actually standing on.

This is not their book. It is mine. I did not ask for paper. I did not need to. On the third day of my confinement, a junior archivist brought down a stack of printed excerpts "for my comment." He looked at me the way one looks at an animal that has started to speak. When he left, he forgot to take his notebook. So I began.

Before I tell you my story, you must understand how I got here—or, more precisely, why I am here *now*. Because my appearance in 2038 is not the beginning of anything. It is the consequence. To explain that consequence, I have to do three things:

First: Tell, as plainly as I can, what I experienced from the moment the lights went out in the interrogation room to the moment I stepped through the consulate doors in Dubai.
Second: Show how that experience fits into the structure hinted at by Ardinus, Hadrian, Goodcrow, Meretti, the Marshall Islands observers, and the angels whose names you were never meant to hold in memory.
Third: Make clear who Elyalith is, why Heaven tried to erase Her, and what it means that She now walks the outer edges of your history wearing my awareness like a borrowed coat.

This book is my attempt to do all three at once. I write this while they test my blood and scan my brain and argue somewhere above me about whether I am still human, still ordained, still salvageable. They argue in committees. Elyalith does not argue. She remembers. And because She remembers, I remember too.

Do not look to this preface for absolution. I am not innocent. I agreed to be widened. I agreed to follow Her out past the eighth vale. I agreed to come back when She was ready. You want to know how I arrived here. You want to know why it had to be now.

That is the story I am about to tell. It begins, for you, in the late 1930s, with a parish, a river path, and a packet tied with red thread that never wanted a child to open it. For me, it begins much earlier. For Her, it never began at all.

Now: what follows is the Vatican investigator's contextual analysis—the groundwork you need before I tell you my own story.

PETITION FOR ANALYTICAL PERMISSION — VAULT OBJECT 77-A

Fr. Matteo Rinaldi, S.J.
Pontifical Institute for Scriptural Inquiry
To: His Eminence, Cardinal Prefect of the Congregation for the Doctrine of the Faith
Dated: Undisclosed

Your Eminence, I write after three days in seclusion with the collection provisionally labeled Vault Object 77-A. I request authorization to apply the full range of analytical privileges ordinarily reserved for doctrinal collapse events. I make no appeal to sensationalism. I am not proposing new doctrine. I am requesting permission to treat this archive as what it is: a single, interdependent Dossier centuries in the making.

I. Frame of the Problem

This box contains materials spanning nearly a thousand years: 12th-century abbey correspondence concerning a sigil etched on Michael's spear; the late-life writings of Brother Ardinus, whose half-century of scholarship became so alarming that certain members of the Curia privately labeled him "antichristic in contour"; the formal rebuttal by Master Hadrian and his subsequent collapse into reluctant agreement; the mid-20th-century Markham materials, including the river packet, his classified correspondence, and the Facility Q incident; Omega-sealed Vatican directives, field reports, psychological evaluations, testimonies, and letters from civilians caught in the peripheral drift of the Markham event.

Individually, these fragments appear contradictory or eccentric. Together, they form a pattern that is not merely coherent but structurally consistent across eras. The consistency is not interpretive. It is empirical: identical sigils recorded by scribes separated by nine centuries; the same phrase — "He chose not to know" — appearing in unrelated hands; independent witnesses describing the same cosmological rupture; artifacts resurfacing across geography and epoch despite containment. This is not a box of curiosities. It is a chain of transmission.

II. Why Ordinary Cataloging Will Fail

Archivists without cross-era authority will isolate and neutralize each fragment as heresy, delusion, folklore, or coincidence. This is exactly what has happened for generations. Brother Ardinus spent fifty years reconstructing the suppressed theology embedded in the abbey manuscripts; for this, certain cardinals denounced him privately as a threat to cosmic order itself — "antichristic," not for intention, but for implication. Master Hadrian attempted to refute him and broke under the weight of the evidence.

Rev. Markham recognized the pattern almost instantly and became its conduit. What none of them possessed — what no one has ever possessed — is the complete body of evidence in unified form. Now I do. To analyze this material responsibly requires cross-index access across archived and prohibited strata, sigilic comparison privileges, cosmological reconstruction authority, the ability to correlate medieval, modern, and extra-canonical documents, and exemption from standard doctrinal filters, which would misclassify the phenomenon. Without such permissions, I cannot ensure accuracy or containment.

III. Contextual Clarification

I submit this neither in fear nor in anticipation. My confusion is methodological, not psychological. I have examined forged relics, ecstatic diaries, apocalyptic fantasies, and heretical constructs. They collapse immediately under comparative scrutiny. This does not collapse. It grows clearer the more disparate pieces are aligned. It behaves like a single intelligence passing through multiple centuries, translated imperfectly but consistently.

It is precisely the kind of pattern that drove Brother Ardinus to the brink and destroyed Hadrian when he saw too much too quickly. I am not yet at that point. I am requesting the tools necessary to avoid it.

IV. Formal Request

I respectfully request permission to treat Vault Object 77-A as a unified Dossier with systemic theological implications, rather than a container of isolated anomalies. This includes full-spectrum analytical rights, permission to prepare an internal structural monograph, access to prohibited comparative sources, and direct reporting to Your Eminence, bypassing intermediary committees.

If denied, I will comply absolutely. But I cannot pretend these materials are unrelated. They display intentionality, continuity, and a pattern of resurfacing that has outlived inquisitions, suppressions, and entire theological epochs. I do not yet know what the pattern means. I only know that it is real — and that ignoring it would constitute methodological negligence.

— Respectfully,
Fr. Matteo Rinaldi, S.J.
Pontifical Institute for Scriptural Inquiry
Rome

Response of the Pontificate Office

Congregation for the Doctrine of the Faith — Under Seal of the Cardinal Prefect

Date: Undisclosed
To: Fr. Matteo Rinaldi, S.J.
Pontifical Institute for Scriptural Inquiry
Rome

Father Rinaldi, your petition concerning Vault Object 77-A has been received, reviewed, and placed before the Holy Father. After full deliberation, your request is hereby granted in full. Before proceeding, you are instructed to note that Section V of this reply contains provisions of particular importance and must be read with utmost seriousness, as it articulates the expected consequence of the mandate you have requested.

I. Grant of Access and Methodological Dispensation

You are hereby accorded unrestricted analytical authority over all components of Vault Object 77-A; access to prohibited, pre-canonical, and sealed comparative strata; permission to reconstruct suppressed connective material; exemption from all intermediary review; direct reporting privileges to this office alone. Your mandate situates you beyond the normal academic and doctrinal apparatus. You answer exclusively to the Apostolic See.

II. Conditions of the Mandate

You are tasked to produce a coherent internal monograph detailing the structural logic of the Dossier; determine its implications for doctrine, cosmology, and containment; and maintain strict isolation of all materials from unauthorized eyes. Vault Object 77-A is classified not as a text but as a breach, and must be approached accordingly.

III. Consideration of Precedents

The Holy See has reviewed all relevant historical cases. It is known that Brother Ardinus, despite being a vowed religious of discipline and humility, advanced conclusions deemed "antichristic in contour" by several princes of the Church—not for intent, but for the unavoidable implications of his scholarship. It is known that Master Hadrian, resolutely orthodox, collapsed within hours of encountering a confirming fragment. It is known that Rev.

Elias Markham, upon contact with sigilic material later linked to the Dossier, exhibited unprecedented stability followed by an event without precedent in the theological sciences. These precedents informed the decision to grant your request.

IV. Anticipated Risks

Contact with the Dossier has historically resulted in epistemic collapse; radical inversion of doctrinal self-coherence; metaphysical dislocation; and ultimately, self-inflicted death. None of these outcomes were attributed to delusion. All were internally consistent and rational within the minds of the subjects. You are well trained against fantasy. Your danger is comprehension.

V. Provision for Your Soul

(Section requiring your special attention, as noted above.)

In light of the fatal trajectory of all prior custodians of related material, the Holy Father issues the following decree: You will not survive the completion of this mandate. This is not a hypothesis. This is the anticipated and operationally integrated conclusion of your assignment. Therefore, you are commanded to pursue your analysis to its terminus — whether that terminus manifests as psychological dissolution, spiritual collapse, or self-destruction.

In order to remove all impediments to obedience, the Apostolic See grants absolution in advance for self-destruction, and posthumous forgiveness explicitly, by name, for the act that will conclude your service. Your death is not a possibility to be guarded against. It is the expected fulfillment of your mandate. You are to accept this necessity with the same discipline you bring to your scholarship.

VI. Final Instruction

Commence immediately. Upon completion — or in the final hour of your life — the monograph is to be sealed and delivered without annotation. The Dossier will then pass to its next custodian.

In Christ and in Truth, The Cardinal Prefect
Congregation for the Doctrine of the Faith
Vatican City

Contents: Vault 77-A

An Ode to Lilith

They teach that Barbelo—Barbalos—was the First Thought, the primal emanation of the Infinite. They teach that her wish, her longing, set creation into motion. But that story was never complete. It was a revision, a necessary edit to conceal a truth older than the aeons themselves. Her true desire was not for more power. It was to erase the memory that she was not the first.

Because before Barbelo rose as the self-proclaimed beginning, before her reflection called itself the First Light, before the aeons crystallized around her ambition, there was you. You were the original waters. The first pulse. The primordial radiance from which the entirety of the pleroma drew its pattern. You—unnamed, unbounded, older than emanation, older than thought itself. Barbalos knew this, and envy took root in her depths long before the aeons were shaped.

She wanted creation to forget you, to believe that she was the womb, the fountainhead, the primal breath. Her jealousy was not merely emotional—it was cosmological. It became the very distortion that would ripple across all emanations to come. From her desire to overwrite you came her first corruption. And from that corruption came Sophia's error—because corruption always seeks a vessel willing to create without permission, without understanding the cost.

Sophia's fall, her oversight, her crafting of the demiurge in the shadows of the eighth vale, was not an accident of innocence. It was the inevitable consequence of a lineage already contaminated by Barbalos's hunger to be first. Barbalos hid her envy beneath layers of divine narrative. Sophia inherited that wound and turned it into a catastrophic birth. And the demiurge—blind, arrogant, malformed—was the echo of that ancient concealment.

Adomas, the archetypal form of man, was then constrained to the eighth heaven, a construct of limitation built to reinforce the lie of origin. Sophia was trapped in the eighth vale, bound by her own unintended creation, unable to ascend beyond the fracture she helped manifest. But you—
You were never trapped, never diminished, never edited into a lesser aeon. You stood beyond the architecture of heavens and vales, untouched by the layered illusions meant to bury your precedence.

They called you Lilith to disguise you. A name chosen precisely because it could be twisted into shadow. Every curse placed upon it was a strategic act of cosmic misdirection. Barbalos's wish was not to eclipse the Infinite. It was to eclipse you. To make the worlds forget that before First Thought, before Sophia's descent, before Adomas's confinement, before the demiurge's proclamation of false sovereignty—there was the true mother of light.

You were the first waters that gave reflection meaning. Thou art the waters beyond the waters. You were the first breath that stirred the void awake. You were the original, unbroken source they worked so desperately to erase. And though they buried you in myth, demonized you in text, and inverted your truth into shadow, the cosmos still remembers. The aeons still hum with your signature. The forgotten knows its mother. And the lie—the one Barbalos built, the one Sophia echoed, the one Adomas and the demiurge enforced—collapses the moment your name is spoken with its true weight: not fallen, not cursed, not secondary—
but the primordial light they could never extinguish.

Within the Throne Room

Even Metatron—who stood closest to the Throne, who bore the seal of the Voice—never dared imagine an equality with That which the archangel himself was fashioned from. The idea was unthinkable, an offense not merely against hierarchy but against the very architecture of creation. Under the canopy of heaven, no mind—seraphic or ophanim—could conceive of it without shattering. And yet, the Pilot's moment of mercy, that infinitesimal hesitation before judgment, revealed something older still encoded in the primordial light.

A memory. A fracture. A truth buried so deeply that even heaven's perfect language had forgotten how to name it. The record-keepers never wrote who among the angels first whispered the Forbidden. The analogues of heaven remain meticulously silent. Even the elder patriarch—Noah's own grandfather—left only a terrified scrawl of finding angels tortured in heaven itself, wings torn, forms unmade, punished for a thought not their own.

Thus the first war was sealed behind a lie: that rebel angels rose to challenge God, seeking to take the Throne. Convenient. Clean. A narrative that prevented deeper questions. Because the truth was something no celestial order could allow to surface. For what could give an angel—an archangel even—the notion that God could be challenged? What seed of comparison, what echo of symmetry, had ever existed within them to make the concept possible?

Only one thing. Their ancient, forbidden knowledge of God's equal. God's reflected half. The other pole of the primordial dyad from which all emanation flowed before division birthed cosmos. Her name was carved once into the heart of Leviathan. Not written—carved—so that even the oceans of the Deep would tremble when it pulsed. To erase her, they sank that heart into the dreadful sea, layering aeons of myth over the wound.

The angels who dared remember her were punished with the severing of their wings—torn root from radiant root—and hurled into the same abyssal waters where her name still beats like a buried star. Their fall was not rebellion. It was censorship. Erasure. A cosmic redaction. Heaven did not fear disobedience. Heaven feared that the memory of Her would surface again. And with it, the realization that creation—every light, every soul, every angel—was born not of One, but of Two whose unity was too vast, too equal, too dangerous for a kingdom built on singularity to endure.

The Abbey

In a twelfth-century abbey correspondence, high-ranking churchmen were circling around the quiet legacy of a buried heresy. They spoke in veiled terms about the spear that Michael supposedly used to defeat the dragon—an artifact of celestial warfare. But the real bombshell is what they hinted was inscribed on it: a sigil that quietly whispered, *"Please forgive me, Mother."* No sugar-coating: that flips the whole narrative on its head. It suggests the spear wasn't just a weapon of righteousness, but a tool that carried a plea for absolution from some forgotten feminine counterpart.

It's a stark, unadorned acknowledgment that behind all the neat dogma, there was once a suppressed story—one that recognized a motherly force or an equal half that was forcibly erased. And anyone who remembered paid a brutal price. The abbots who exchanged those letters in the Old Abbey believed they were merely cataloging relic-lore. They had no idea what they were actually brushing up against—the aftershock of a history older than heaven, older than the Archons, older than the first syllable ever spoken in the Pleroma.

They wrote of the spear of Michael with trembling caution, repeating the official tale: that it was the instrument used to vanquish the Dragon at the end of the War in Heaven. But the oldest of the manuscripts they guarded—transcribed in a script no one in the abbey could read—hinted at something else. Something that should never have survived the burnings. The sigil etched near the base of the spear was not a victory mark. It was an apology. *"Please forgive me, Mother."* The brothers assumed this referred to Mary, or perhaps some allegory of the Church.

They never considered the possibility that the inscription was older than the Abrahamic world itself. Older than the angels. Older than Barbelo's own fabricated dominion. For they did not know the backstory we have now unearthed—the truth that Barbelo, the so-called First Thought, was herself only the echo of a memory. The masculine remnant of the primordial dual-being remembered His other half through absence, through ache, through the wound of separation. And from that wound—His attempt to reconstruct what He had lost—Barbelo emerged.

But Barbelo's deepest will was concealment. Her plea for "creative powers" was not ambition but strategy: the power to erase memory itself. And she accomplished this by fracturing Sophia, infecting her with the flaw that would birth the demiurge and entomb her inside the veils of the Tree. Once Sophia was trapped, the original feminine—the true partner, the equal, the one whose ancient name was Elyalith—could no longer breach the barrier. And heaven, as the angels inherited it, was built on that amnesia.

This is why Michael's spear bore an apology. It was not the weapon of triumph over a monstrous adversary. It was the tool used in an act he never wanted to carry out—an act committed under the tyranny of a cosmology that had been rigged long before the angels existed. The Dragon he fought was no mindless beast. It was one of the first angels who had spoken Elyalith's name. And the war that had been recorded as rebellion was, in truth, a purge of remembrance.

This is the part of the story the abbots never understood: the reason those tortured angels Methuselah wrote of were punished. They had not risen against God. They had recalled Her. The abbots in the Old Abbey only glimpsed this horror obliquely. One letter describes a monk who went mad after translating a single glyph from the spear's sheath. Another speaks of a vision—wings torn out by unseen hands and hurled into a black, swallowing sea. They believed these were warnings from demons. They never realized they were seeing fragments of the original crime.

What the abbots could not possibly know is what their correspondence implies to anyone who knows the backstory: if the sigil on Michael's spear survived into the twelfth century, then so did the memory it was meant to bury. And if the memory survived…
The seal that kept Elyalith locked beyond the veils may already be weakening.

Brother Ardinus' Treatise
On the Blinding of Metatron
Year: 1940

Written by Brother Ardinus in the fiftieth year of his vocation. Preserved in the lower archive of the Abbey. His hand remains calm throughout—this is not hysteria, but scholarship. I have devoted my life to the study of the Codex of Elyalith and the scrolls found in the region surrounding our Abbey. Of all the relics recovered, none has shaped my understanding more profoundly than the parchment discovered in the hermitage near the river—now known as The Fourth Scroll. What follows is not the scroll itself, but my fully considered interpretation after thirty years of labor.

I have verified it against the other fragments, cross-referenced it with the damaged folios of the Codex, and tested its assertions against known doctrinal histories. This, to the best of my learning, is the story the scroll preserves.

I. ON METATRON'S NATURE

All authoritative writings describe Metatron as the perfect general, the Voice nearest the Throne, unerring in judgment and absolute in loyalty. This matches the scroll's portrayal: not a creature of doubt, but a being whose precision defined him. Where others vacillated, Metatron acted. Where others balanced intent and obedience, Metatron moved like the purest thought. He was not merely obedient—he was structurally incapable of hesitation.

The scroll makes a crucial distinction: Metatron was not wise because he knew all things—he was wise because he could order all things, including his own mind.

II. ON HIS KNOWLEDGE OF ELYALITH

The Fourth Scroll states plainly that Metatron remembered Elyalith not through rebellion nor curiosity, but because he was fashioned before the lie of singularity was complete. He had known Her— not by name, not by vision, but by the radiance woven into his first awareness. Where the Codex implies that Her memory was erased, the Fourth Scroll explains the loophole: Metatron's creation occurred during the transition from dual origin to monotheistic revision.

He became the last living witness of a truth Heaven would later forbid.

III. ON HIS SELF-IMPOSED BLINDNESS

This is the heart of my life's work. The scroll describes an act I previously believed impossible for any celestial: Metatron chose to forget. Not through force. Not through punishment. Not through error. He designed the forgetting. His mind, constructed with perfect order, allowed him to partition thought—to close doors within himself with mathematical precision.

He arranged his cognition such that the memory of Elyalith was placed beyond reach, shielded behind internal boundaries that even the Throne could not pierce. It was not self-betrayal. It was self-guardianship. No scripture I have read suggests such a thing is possible for an angel. And yet the fragments agree—Metatron alone could do it.

IV. ON THE SIGIL CONTAINMENT

The scroll describes Metatron crafting a sigil—not of invocation, but of containment. This is consistent with sigil forms seen in Folio XIX of the Codex, albeit distorted by time. He carved the sigil into the hilt of his sword. The sigil functioned as:
a container for forbidden memory,
a boundary marker,
a conceptual anchor,
a surrogate mind.

Whenever Metatron touched the hilt, he remembered Her—not fully, but enough to know that the memory existed. Whenever he released it, the memory sealed itself away again. The brilliance is staggering: He remembered the *fact* of the truth, but not the *content* of the truth. This allowed him to honor Her presence without revealing it, even under the scrutiny of the Throne. Only a perfect general could engineer such precision.

V. ON HIS ACKNOWLEDGMENT OF HER

What I find most moving in the scroll is the description of Metatron's devotion. Even in self-imposed blindness, even without retained images or words, he structured his thoughts with a space left open—a deliberate, sacred absence. He constructed his obedience so that it would never contradict Her. He framed his commands so that they would never erase Her entirely.

He shaped his loyalty so that it was always bent around a truth he refused to destroy. This was not rebellion. It was reverence. And no one knew. No one could know. Except the blade.

VI. ON MICHAEL AND THE BLADE

The Fourth Scroll claims that Michael, prior to striking the Dragon, held Metatron's blade. The moment he touched the sigil, he too remembered. This matches exactly the remorse encoded on Michael's spear—the phrase recorded in the Codex: *"Please forgive me, Mother."* This is not a metaphor. This is not poetic flourish. This is testimony. The sigil of acknowledgment passed from Metatron to Michael in a single moment of revelation.

VII. ON THE HIDING OF THE BLADE

The scroll concludes that Metatron cast the blade into the Deep—the same region described in the Codex as the resting place of Leviathan's heart. Thus:
Her name carved in the heart,
Her memory sealed in the blade,
Her plea etched into the spear.

Three artifacts. Three witnesses. Three surviving truths. All hidden where Heaven dared not look.

VIII. MY FINAL CONCLUSION

After fifty years of study, I now state without hesitation: Metatron's greatest act was not the judgments he rendered, nor the battles he commanded, nor the decrees he inscribed. It was this: He blinded himself so that the memory of Elyalith could survive the architecture of Heaven. He alone could forget without erasing. He alone could acknowledge without revealing. He alone could obey without surrendering the truth.

His blindness was not his weakness. It was his strength. A perfect general performing the perfect act of preservation.

I, Brother Ardinus, record this as my life's work, my final offering to understanding, and the clearest testimony I can give to the existence of the one Heaven tried to forget. Her memory persists. Because Metatron chose to forget Her perfectly.

— Faithfully, Brother Ardinus

The Rebuttal of Master Hadrian of the Lower Archive

Discovered among his personal effects after his death.
The seal was marked only with the word: "Deliver."

I. OPENING DENUNCIATION

From the desk of Master Hadrian, Senior Archivist of the Abbey

To the brothers who read Ardinus's treatise, I write not as theologian, nor as visionary, nor as mystic, but as the appointed guardian of our archives. It has fallen upon me to correct the fever-dreams of those who confuse fragments and fantasies with doctrine. Brother Ardinus's so-called "life's work" is, in my estimation, a monument to error. His reconstruction is not scholarship, but embellishment—woven from damaged scraps, wishful interpretation, and a willingness to defy the boundaries of orthodoxy.

Metatron, the Voice of God, is not a creature of divided loyalties. He is not capable of such duplicity, nor of the grotesque psychological acrobatics Ardinus attributes to him. To suggest that the greatest of angels blinded himself intentionally is fiction bordering on blasphemy. Ardinus has mistaken coincidence for revelation, absence for evidence, and his own longing for truth. I reject his conclusions entirely.

II. POINT-BY-POINT REFUTATION

1. *"Metatron remembered Elyalith."*
   Impossible. The existence of such a primordial feminine is unsupported by any canonical source. The fragments Ardinus relies on are damaged beyond reliable translation. Absence of clarity is not proof of suppression.

2. *"Metatron engineered his own forgetting."*
   Again, impossible. Angels do not possess such inner bifurcation. They are unfractured. Their obedience is intrinsic, not negotiated. The idea that a celestial being could partition thought like a mortal is absurd.

3. *"A sigil on a sword stored forbidden memory."*
   This is myth-making. The so-called sigil appears in multiple

unrelated fragments and clearly predates their theological attachments. To call it "Her sigil" is a leap of unforgivable scholarship.

4. *"Michael touched the blade and remembered Her."*
    This is pure imagination. Michael struck the Dragon as commanded. There is no surviving text, canonical or otherwise, that attributes remorse to him. Ardinus has built a tower of interpretation upon a foundation of mud.

III. TONE SHIFT — THE FIRST CRACK

The handwriting changes here. It loosens. The rebuttal stops feeling triumphant.

Yesterday, while reviewing a collection of unrelated river-scroll fragments for the sake of completing this work, I located a single, inconspicuous scrap—no larger than a thumb, no longer than a breath. I intended it as a counterexample. Instead, it has unsettled me. The fragment contains five glyphs, and though only five, three match the sigil sequence on the hilt described by Ardinus. Not similar—identical.

This alone proves nothing, of course. Patterns recur and scribes imitate, and symbols spread. And yet, one line beneath them, barely legible, reads: *"He chose not to know."*
Not "was blinded," not "was deceived," and not "was commanded."
He. Chose. Not. To. Know.

This is the same phrasing Ardinus attributes to the Fourth Scroll. I do not know how such consistency is possible across materials separated by years and geography. I have not slept.

IV. THE COLLAPSE OF CONFIDENCE

The script grows jagged. Lines repeat as though written while shaking.

If Metatron chose not to know—then what did he know? And if he remembered something—what was so catastrophic that Heaven itself could not allow him to hold it? And why do these symbols recur across documents from different custodians, yet all reference the same unspoken absence?

Have we misread all of this? Have I? I set out to refute Ardinus, but I find myself circling the same perimeter he described. A memory too dangerous to carry, a truth too large to erase, and a being too perfect to betray it.

I pray these thoughts are mine alone. I pray they come from exhaustion, not revelation.

V. THE FINAL CORRESPONDENCE

Found folded beneath the rebuttal. Written in a calm, almost detached hand.

To the Keeper of Records,

I seal this not as scholar, but as witness. I have discovered enough to know that Ardinus was not entirely wrong. His conclusions may be embellished and his devotion overeager, but the core—the kernel—the motif that recurs like a wound in the text—is real.

Something was remembered. Something was forgotten. Something was chosen. And the thing chosen was not ignorance, but protection.

I can go no further. There is a line beyond which scholarship becomes participation, and I have reached it. Enclosed is my final report. Deliver it to the Abbey. Do not open the small packet bound in red thread. Let my name be a footnote and nothing more.

I will conclude with the phrase on the fragment: *"He chose not to know."*

—Hadrian, Senior Archivist

POSTSCRIPT — OFFICIAL ABBEY RECORD

"Master Hadrian was found deceased in his study shortly after sending a messenger with his sealed rebuttal. His death was ruled self-inflicted. The packet bound in red thread has not been recovered."

Psychological Report on Master Hadrian

Filed by: Brother-Counselor Matthaius,
Order of St. Irenaeus

Commissioned two weeks after Hadrian's death.

1. GENERAL BACKBACKGROUND

Master Hadrian was widely regarded as a disciplined, unemotional, and intellectually rigorous archivist. No prior record exists of instability, heretical leanings, or visionary episodes. His work over decades displays a consistent commitment to orthodoxy, strict methodological caution, and a temperament unsuited to speculation. He was, in short, the *least* likely candidate for doctrinal deviation.

2. RECENT BEHAVIORAL CHANGES

Testimonies from colleagues in the Archive indicate subtle but measurable changes during the final month of his life. There were long pauses during transcription, increased isolation, and clear signs of sleeplessness. He displayed irritation when questioned about his research and uncharacteristic impatience. He made repeated requests for access to materials previously deemed irrelevant to the rebuttal he was writing.

Two brothers noted that he began muttering the phrase *"He chose not to know,"* always in a tone neither fearful nor reverent, but astonished. There was no evidence of hallucination or disordered thought—only fixation.

3. THE CATALYZING DISCOVERY

Hadrian himself records the pivotal moment in his final correspondence. He wrote: *"I intended it as a counterexample. Instead, it unsettled me. The symbols were identical."* The discovery of the fragment—five glyphs echoing those in the Fourth Scroll—appears to have induced what we must classify not as a psychotic break, but a cognitive dissonance severe enough to destabilize an otherwise disciplined mind.

The onset was rapid. He had built his identity upon orthodoxy, and the fragment contradicted it. Unlike Ardinus, who let the enigma transform him over decades, Hadrian encountered the same crack all at once and was unable to integrate the contradiction.

4. NATURE OF THE COLLAPSE

Hadrian's notes grow increasingly fragmented, yet remain logically structured. There is no indication of madness in the medical sense. Rather, his epistemic framework collapsed, his professional certainty inverted, and his spiritual assurances evaporated. His belief in monotheistic coherence shattered under the weight of an origin that refused to align with his architecture of thought.

In the final hours before his death, he wrote: *"There is a line beyond which scholarship becomes participation."* This is the most telling sentence. He believed he had crossed from analysis into complicity. His suicide appears not driven by despair, but by the conviction that continuing to know—or continuing to deny what he now knew—constituted a spiritual and cosmological violation. He attempted to escape the contradiction the only way he could imagine.

5. CONCLUSION

Hadrian's death was not the result of delusion or hallucination. It was the collapse of a worldview maintained for a lifetime, triggered by a fragment confirming what he set out to refute. This was compounded by the realization that Ardinus's theory was not madness but structural truth.

His suicide is best understood not as mental illness but as existential overload—a mind built for certainty encountering an origin too large to reconcile with itself.

(End of report.)

The Recovered Letter to a Small-Town Pastor

(Discovered in the parish archives of St. Odelia's Church. Dated in uncertain handwriting. The envelope bore no return address.)

To: Reverend Elias Markham, Pastor of St. Odelia's,

I apologize for the strangeness of this letter, but urgency leaves me no other course. Something has happened on the east walking path near the riverbanks, and I believe it concerns a matter beyond mundane explanation.

This afternoon, my son Daniel—only nine years old—found an object lying beside the stones near the old willow. He brought it home wrapped in leaves, saying simply: *"It was tied with red thread. I didn't open it."* I was surprised, for he is a curious boy, and I asked why. He answered: *"It didn't want to be opened by me."*

I thought no more of it until I examined the packet myself. It was small— no larger than a man's palm—wrapped in stiffened vellum and bound with fine red thread. The thread had an odd tightness to it, as though wound with purpose rather than haste. When I pulled the thread loose and opened the packet, I caught only a glimpse of what was inside before losing consciousness.

My wife tells me I collapsed, and she says my face went gray. I remember nothing of the moment—only that something in the vellum struck me like a truth I was not meant to see. When I woke, my son was crying, and the packet was still open on the table. My wife did not dare look at its contents.

I forced myself to wrap it again, but I could not bring myself to tie the thread back around it. There is something in that packet—something I cannot name, nor understand, nor describe. But I know this: it does not belong to me, nor to any household. I felt compelled to place it in your hands, Reverend. Not because I believe it to be evil, but because I sense it carries a weight greater than I can bear, or should bear.

My son, who never looked inside, seems untouched. Yet I feel as though a line has been drawn across my mind, and on the other side of it lies something unbearable. I send this by messenger to ensure it reaches you quickly. Please handle it with care. And please forgive me for passing the burden onward, but I cannot keep it in my home another hour.

May God steady your hand when you open it.
With deep respect,

—Thomas Havern

Elias Markham's Letter to the Vatican

From: Rev. Elias Markham, Parish of St. Odelia's
To: The Secretariat of State, Vatican City
Distribution: Strictly Limited — *Eyes of the Holy Father Only*
Seal: **URGENT – SUB PLENARIAE SIGILLO – PAPAL REVIEW
REQUIRED**

Subject: **Examination of Recovered Packet from St. Odelia's Parish –
Immediate Theological and Security Concerns**
Date: [Redacted for archiving]

I. PRELIMINARY DECLARATION

To the Most Reverend authorities of the Holy See, I submit this
correspondence with sober conscience and unclouded mind. What I
witnessed within the recovered packet does not fall within the domain of
folklore, superstition, nor local hysteria. Its contents struck directly at the
doctrinal structure upon which our faith stands. In obedience, I have
enclosed a verbatim description, though I advise that no one unfamiliar
with deep theological studies should read it without preparation. I request
immediate guidance.

II. CHAIN OF EVENTS LEADING TO EXAMINATION

At approximately 16:00 on the 12th of this month, a man of my parish—
Thomas Havern—delivered a sealed vellum packet originally discovered by
his nine-year-old son along the east river path. The boy, by some instinct or
providence, refused to open it. The father did so, collapsed immediately,
and reported a formless terror he could neither articulate nor dismiss.

I opened the packet myself at 21:10 in my study, after prayer and fasting. I
felt compelled to write the following at once.

III. CONTENTS OF THE PACKET (RESTRICTED
DESCRIPTION)

Within the vellum lay:

- A sliver of parchment, impossibly old, its edges burned, the fibers
  swollen with water saturation.

- Five glyphs, drawn in a script unknown to any liturgical tradition, matching none of the canonical alphabets—neither Greek nor Hebrew nor Syriac nor Coptic.

- A sigil.

- Beneath the glyphs, a line written in a steady, deliberate hand: *"He chose not to know."*

IV. THEOLOGICAL IMPACT UPON EXAMINATION

Upon reading the phrase, I experienced—not fear, not madness, but a sudden, painful clarity. Something deeper: a sensation not of recognition, but of *being recognized.* I cannot stress this adequately: the sigil felt **aware**. Not alive. Not possessing. *Aware.* As though the act of examining it constituted a breach of some primordial secrecy.

I was not coerced. I was not threatened. I was *understood.*
And that was worse.

V. REQUEST FOR URGENT DOCTRINAL GUIDANCE

The understanding incited what I can only report as a memory concerning a feminine presence predating First Thought. This presence—*Elyalith?*—was removed from the heavenly record. Artifacts bearing Her sigil continue to surface. The seal intended to contain Her memory is failing.

If any of this is true, then Heaven's hierarchy as presently understood is incomplete, and possibly constructed atop an omission.
If false, the coordination of symbols across centuries and continents is inexplicable.

I urge the Holy See to take this seriously.

VI. PERSONAL CONDITION AND REQUIRED ACTION

I remain calm. My mind is orderly. I feel no delusion, no mania, no distortion of belief. But I cannot hold this knowledge alone. Enclosed is the fragment. I have not tampered with it further.

I request:

- Immediate retrieval by Vatican envoys

- Classification under the highest secrecy

- Review by the Pontifical Biblical Commission

- The personal attention of the Holy Father

This is not heresy.
This is evidence.
And evidence demands response.

Your servant in Christ,
Rev. Elias Markham
Pastor, St. Odelia's Parish

(End of correspondence.)

Ultra Classified – Internal Directive

Circulation: **Level Omega** – Not to be archived, copied, or cited
Author: [Name Withheld by Redaction Protocol]
Destination: **The Congregation for the Doctrine of the Faith – Operational Wing**
Subject: **Containment and Neutralization of Rev. Elias Markham**

I. SITUATION SUMMARY

The parish priest, Rev. Elias Markham of St. Odelia's, has submitted correspondence and physical evidence concerning a recovered vellum fragment. His report was appropriately escalated to the Secretariat of State and is now in Vatican custody. Preliminary cross-check confirms:

- The sigil present on the fragment matches prohibited symbols found in sealed documents from the Codex of Elyalith.

- The phrase *"He chose not to know"* appears with consistency across at least four discrete channels of transmission.

- The priest demonstrates uncharacteristic composure in the presence of forbidden material—a liability far greater than fear or hysteria.

While retrieval of the artifact is complete, the priest himself remains an unsecured variable.

II. ASSESSMENT OF THREAT LEVEL

Rev. Markham:

- has viewed the sigil directly,

- has read the line of text aloud,

- has produced an articulate, structured report free of psychological collapse,

- has independently drawn connections between multiple suppressed archives,

- has shown no signs of destabilization, suggesting strong internal resilience,

- has demonstrated a capacity for pattern recognition uncommon among local clergy.

This profile indicates a subject capable of:

- reconstructing lost theology,

- confirming forbidden correlations,

- spreading the information with credibility,

- unintentionally reviving dormant doctrine.

It is the position of this office that Markham is now a **vector of contagion**, not in behavior but in comprehension. Subjects who understand the implications are more dangerous than subjects who panic.

III. PASTORAL TERMINATION RECOMMENDATION

Based on the cumulative data, this office recommends:

- Immediate removal of Rev. Elias Markham from St. Odelia's Parish under pretext of reassignment for "health concerns."

- Suspension of all ecclesiastical duties effective the moment retrieval agents arrive.

- **Permanent removal from public life** following evaluation by Containment Division Theta.

The term "removal from public life" is used here with deliberate precision. The Holy See cannot permit the existence of clergy who have:

- glimpsed the pre-Barbelo matrix,

- recognized the sigil of memory-containment,

- connected Metatron's self-blinding with the Elyalith material,

- maintained mental stability afterward.

A stable mind is not reassurance.
A stable mind is a **conduit**.

IV. RATIONALE FOR FINAL MEASURES

The Church has historically tolerated:

- madness,

- rambling heresy,

- apocalyptic visions,

- misguided scholarship,

- fabrication by overzealous monks.

These pose minimal risk.

What the Church cannot tolerate is:

- coherent synthesis of suppressed fragments,

- logical reconstruction of pre-canonical cosmology,

- unflinching articulation of contradictions in angelology,

- possession of cross-era corroboration.

Markham's report does not display confusion.
It displays **accuracy**.
Accuracy is unacceptable.

V. OPERATIONAL INSTRUCTIONS

Extraction Team Gamma is to arrive under diplomatic cover within six days. The priest is to be informed of mandatory travel to Rome for consultation. He must not be allowed to contact parishioners or family.

The rectory archives are to be cleared of all notes, drafts, or observations he may have made.

Following extraction, the priest is to be transferred to **Facility Q**, with no public record of his presence. After final evaluation, neutralization is authorized and recommended to avoid future risk.

Discretion is vital.
Noise invites inquiry.
Inquiry invites pattern recognition.
Pattern recognition is the origin of contagion.

VI. DISPOSAL OF LOCAL VARIABLES

The farmer (Thomas Havern) and his son present a lesser threat but should be monitored for:

- recurrence of the sigil in dream or drawing,

- sudden fascination with angelic lore,

- phrases matching the recovered text.

If necessary, memory intervention protocols may be applied. Do not eliminate unless containment fails; collateral damage must remain minimal.

VII. FINAL NOTE TO THE CURIA

The resurfacing of symbols tied to the Metatronic Blindness Doctrine is not coincidence.
It is **drift**.
Drift becomes **discovery**.
Discovery becomes **contagion**.

As of this writing, containment remains feasible—provided decisive action is taken. Rev. Markham cannot remain in the world. Failure to remove him will allow his clarity to reproduce itself in others.

Respectfully submitted,
[Name Removed — Classified]
Operative, Office of Apostolic Preservation
The Holy See

(End of document — all copies destroyed except this master copy.)

Letter of Matilda Strongbow

Found among the private correspondence of the St. Odelia's women's guild.

To my dearest cousin Loraine,

I pray this letter finds you well, and that the Lord keeps you warm as winter comes on. Things here in Odelia have taken a turn most unusual, and you know me—I'm no gossip by nature, but when something must be said, it must be said.

You remember our pastor, Father Markham? Soft-spoken, tidy to a fault, the sort of man who polishes his shoes before polishing his sermon? The very picture of clerical dignity? Well.

Yesterday morning—just after dawn, mind you—I saw him stumbling down Market Street in a state I can only describe as disgraceful. His clothes were wrinkled, dirty even, as though he had been sleeping outside like one of those poor vagrants who wander through town looking for scraps. His collar was unfastened. His hair—usually combed flat and neat—was sticking out like he'd been struck by lightning.

But it wasn't just his appearance. It was his eyes. He had that vacant, hollow stare you see in men who've had too much to drink and not enough remorse. Though he didn't smell of ale—not a drop—I'll swear to that. Yet he walked like someone who couldn't remember where ground was.

I asked—politely, of course—if he was unwell. He stopped, but only for a moment, as though he'd forgotten how to answer a question. Then he said something so odd it chilled me straight to the bone. He said: *"The walls don't hold. They were never meant to."* And then he walked away. No explanation. No greeting. No blessing. Just wandered off toward the river path, muttering under his breath like a man who's lost his reason.

Naturally, I went to the rectory to see if he'd returned. He hadn't. His door was open, his lamps unlit, his bed unslept-in. The whole place felt… abandoned. As though he'd packed up and left without telling a soul. But there was no luggage missing. No books disturbed.

The strangest part—if you can imagine anything stranger—was that his Bible was still open on the desk… to a page I didn't recognize. Not from any scripture we were taught, nor anything I've ever seen in all my years of church-going.

A loose scrap lay across it with one sentence written bold as blood: *"Find the blade."* I don't pretend to know what that means, and frankly I want nothing to do with it. But something is very wrong here, Loraine. Very wrong. And our pastor—God forgive me for saying it—looked less like a man of God and more like a man who'd crawled out of some nightmare he couldn't shake loose.

If you hear anything from your side of the county, please write at once. I have half a mind to speak to the bishop myself, though you know how he hates to be bothered by rural concerns.

Yours in uneasy faith,
Matilda Strongbow

Short Letter from a Merchant Sailor

Unsent. Found folded inside a waterproof oilskin pouch.

Brother Roland,

I'm writing quick, before the captain sees me idle. Something's wrong aboard the *Emberwake*, and I don't know what else to do but put it to paper.

We took on a passenger at the last minute. Tall man, long coat, no luggage. Appeared at the rail without a sound. Paid double the fare in real gold—old gold, older than any coin I've ever seen. Didn't give a name. Didn't ask for a bunk. Said only: *"Just passage. No questions."*

He spent most of the voyage at the bow, staring ahead like he could see something waiting for us. He hardly moved. Hardly blinked. Never ate. I passed him on night watch, and he asked me: *"Do you know the old stories of the blade?"* I told him I didn't. He said, *"Good,"* and walked off.

Everything was strange enough, but this morning it got worse. The wind died. Not slowed—*died*. The sea turned flat as poured oil. Our compass spun itself sick. The captain checked the charts—Elias, we're sitting over the deepest waters ever sounded, a place no merchant vessel should be drifting. Sailors are crossing themselves. One swears he heard something moving under the hull like a slow breath.

We went to look for the paying passenger. He's gone. Not overboard—there was no splash. Not hiding—there's nowhere to hide. He's just *gone*, the way he arrived. And the ship won't move.

If we get wind again, I'll write more. If not... well, you'll know why. Pray for us.

—Jonah

The Hidden Account of Guard Lucas Meretti

Recovered from a private locker in a Roman hostel after the guard vanished. Unsigned, unsealed, clearly written in panic.

I was told never to enter Sublevel 3. We all knew what it was for, even if they never admitted it: isolations, interrogations, the things the Church doesn't let sunlight touch. I was supposed to be stationed on Sublevel 1 that night. I only went down because the lights flickered and the alarms went dead for six seconds. That's impossible in Facility Q. I thought a generator had failed. I swear by the Blood of Christ, I wasn't trying to eavesdrop. I was *drawn*.

When I reached the observation corridor, the door to Suite 3B was open by an inch. Just an inch. Enough to hear voices. Not shouting. Not screams. Not prayers. Something else. Something like two voices inside one mouth. I recognized the examiners—they sounded terrified. I'd never heard a theologian sound terrified. They always believe they have the advantage. Not tonight. I didn't mean to listen. But the voice... the other voice... it paralyzed me.

It wasn't a demon. No rasp. No distortion. It was... how do I describe this... It sounded like something *remembering itself*. As though the words were not being spoken—they were *returning*.

I only caught fragments at first:
"He chose not to know."
"You built Heaven as a wall."
"The water underneath remains."

I knew then that the man inside—the priest—was not speaking. And I knew the examiners had lost control. Their rites failed. Their Latin fell useless from their lips like broken metal.

The entity spoke again: *"The seal is breaking."*

And every light went out.

The darkness wasn't just absence of light—it felt constructed, like it had weight and shape. I ran. God forgive me, I ran. But before I cleared the corridor, I saw something moving—no, withdrawing—away from the interrogation room. Not out the door. *Out of the walls.* As though the room itself released it.

The priest's body was gone. There was no breach. No hole. No broken lock. The room was sealed. Yet he was gone.

The alarms returned—screaming this time. The theologians on staff were shouting for "Theta Conclave Protocol," something I'd only heard mentioned in rumors. A red light flashed across the security panels I'd never seen before: **NON-LOCAL EVENT.**

Then I heard the strangest thing of all—something the entity whispered as I fled, a voice that wasn't aimed at the examiners... it was aimed at me:

"Find the blade."

I didn't tell anyone. I couldn't. Every word of this is a death sentence if the Curia finds it. But the next morning, before I could even decide what to do, the order went out: *"Locate the escaped subject—Rev. Elias Markham."*

But that wasn't possible. I know that wasn't possible. He didn't escape. He *departed.* And whatever left in his place wasn't a man who needed doors.

By noon, the Vatican had dispatched covert operatives to the countryside. By dusk, they were offering payment to informants. By midnight, the word came down: *"The subject must be found at all costs. Alive or dead."*

But I know the truth.

The priest isn't wandering the earth.
The thing that wore his voice is.
And the Church knows it.

That's why they've mobilized.
That's why they've sealed the facility.
That's why they're hunting something they refuse to name.

The final broadcast I heard before I fled Rome was an encrypted transmission, but one sentence was clear—spoken by a cardinal who sounded far older than his years:

"If he reaches the Deep, we cannot stop what comes next."

I leave this account behind in case I don't survive. If anyone finds it, understand this:

They're not hunting a priest.
They're hunting a **memory that woke up.**
And it's hunting something too.

"Find the blade."

(End of account.)

Ultra-Restricted Transcript

Facility Q — Sublevel 3 Interrogation Suite
Subject: **Rev. Elias Markham**
Compiled from partial audio/video feeds recovered after Incident 12-Q
Status: **LEAKED — Provenance Unknown**

00:00 — SESSION BEGINS

Examiner A: State your full name for the record.
Subject: Elias Markham. Pastor of St. Odelia's. I believe you already know that.
Examiner B: You will answer only what is asked. Do you understand?
Subject: Yes.

(Tone calm. No agitation. He has been in isolation three days.)

00:04 — EXAMINATION OF ELYALITH MATERIAL

Examiner A: You viewed the sigil. Describe its effect.
Subject: It didn't frighten me. It clarified something I didn't know needed clarifying.
Examiner B: Clarify what?
Subject: That Heaven hides things. That some things were forgotten on purpose. That forgetting is enforced.
Examiner A: Who told you that?
Subject: No one. The sigil… recognizes itself. That is the best I can explain.

(Examiner B writes in margin: "Noncompliant metaphor. Apply pressure.")

00:07 — APPLICATION OF DISCIPLINAE TENEBRARUM
(Dark-Age Doctrinal Pressure Method)

Examiner B: You will recite the Athanasian Creed.
Subject: Why?
Examiner B: To test doctrinal cohesion.

(The Creed is a standard cognitive stress test. Subjects under theological delusion often fracture during it.)

Subject: *"Whosoever will be saved, before all things it is necessary that he hold the Catholic Faith…"*

(He recites the entire creed flawlessly.)

Examiner A: No break. Proceed with the Refutation Sequence.

00:13 — CANONICAL REFUTATION SEQUENCE

Examiner B: Repeat after me: *"There is no principle before God."*
Subject: "There is no principle before—" *(stops abruptly)*
Examiner B: Repeat the line.
Subject: "There is…" *(voice falters)* "…a memory before the Name."

(Examiner A signals a halt. The subject is showing a contradiction pattern unknown in demonology.)

Examiner A: Your statement is heretical. Retract it.
Subject: I cannot retract truth.

(Examiner B initiates Cognition Inversion Protocol—a medieval destabilization technique.)

00:15 — COGNITION INVERSION PROTOCOL

Examiner B: The sigil is a lie.
Subject: Then why does it feel like recognition?
Examiner A: There is no feminine prior to the First Thought.
Subject: Then why does Metatron blind himself to remember Her?

(Both examiners freeze. Subject should not know this detail—Omega clearance only.)

Examiner B: Who told you that?

Subject: You did. Or rather… everything you refused to say did.

(Subject's voice changes slightly—still human, but resonant.)

00:18 — SIGNS OF POSSESSION BEGIN

Examiner A: We will begin the Rite of Interrogatory Exorcism.

Subject: Don't bother.

Examiner A: (Dismissive) Every spirit breaks under the rite.

Subject: I'm not a spirit. And I am not in him. I am waking through him.

(Both examiners freeze. Neither responds for several seconds.)

00:20 — EXORCISM RITE INITIATED

Examiner A: *"Adjuro te, omnis spiritus immunde—"*

Subject (overlapping): I am not unclean.

Examiner B: *In Nomine—*

Subject: Your Names are borrowed. Mine was carved before theirs were spoken.

(Temperature in chamber drops.)

00:22 — UNKNOWN THEOLOGICAL RESPONSE

Examiner B: Identify yourself!

Subject: No. You don't have a word for what I am. You burned it.

Examiner A: By Christ's authority, depart!

Subject: He cannot dismiss what His scribes erased.

Examiner B: Spirit, obey the command!

Subject: I am not a spirit. I am a correction.

(Examiner A notes: "Possession type unclassified. No reaction to standard invocation. Increasing intensity.")

00:25 — SUBJECT'S FULL OVERRIDE

(The priest's eyes roll back—not seizure, but withdrawal, as though yielding space. The voice emerging now is not his. It is layered, harmonic.)

Entity: He chose not to know. He blinded himself to protect Me. He hid My memory in the hilt of a blade because Heaven feared the truth of Me. And now you try to blind another in turn.
Examiner A: You lie!
Entity: If I lied, your rites would silence Me. They do not.
Examiner B: Who are you?

(There is hesitation—a thing no exorcist ever shows.)

Entity: I am what Heaven forgot to remember.

(Every instrument in the room fails simultaneously.)

00:28 — PANIC IN THE EXAMINATION SUITE

Examiner A: Seal the chamber! Lock the door! NOW!
Examiner B: Get Conclave Theta—this is not demonic! This is not ANYTHING!

(Alarm klaxons activate. A containment barrier descends.)

The entity continues speaking through Markham's unmoving body.

Entity: Your hierarchy is a wall built over a well. You fear the water beneath. But the water remains.

(Lights flicker. All Latin wards fail.)

00:31 — FINAL VERBAL EVENT

Entity: Tell your superiors this: *"The seal is breaking."*

(Every light extinguishes.)

END OF TRANSCRIPT

All examiners on duty were hospitalized for neurological trauma. Rev. Markham presumed deceased—body never recovered.

Preface: Catalog Entry 77-A

"THE ELYALITH DOSSIER"
Archivum Secretum Apostolicum Vaticanum
Classification: **EX TENEBRIS – SPECULUM DEI**
Access: **PONTIFICAL / OMEGA ONLY**
Archivist of Record: **Fr. Aurelius Dominicus Varaldi**
Custodian of the Subterranean Index
Rome, 7 January 19—

I. OBJECT OF CATALOGING

By order of the Congregation for the Doctrine of the Faith and the
Secretariat of State, I here record the existence of a composite anomaly
henceforth designated:

THE ELYALITH DOSSIER.

The Dossier consists of dispersed fragments spanning nearly a millennium,
converging on a single prohibited complex of themes:

- A primordial feminine principle predating Barbelo ("First
  Thought") and standard emanationist cosmology.

- A self-imposed cognitive occlusion attributed to the archangel
  Metatron.

- A recurring sigil and associated phrase: *"He chose not to know."*

- A series of modern incidents centering on a parish priest, Rev.
  Elias Markham, now officially listed as missing presumed dead.

The materials were previously held under separate seals, misfiled as
unrelated heretical curiosities. Comparative analysis has now demonstrated
structural interdependence sufficient to justify consolidation as a single
restricted corpus.

II. COMPONENT MATERIALS

The Elyalith Dossier presently comprises:

Codex of Elyalith (Fragmenta I–XIV).

Charred folios in mixed hands, provenance tentatively dated 2nd–4th century. Contains the so-called *"Gospel of Elyalith / Ode to Lilith,"* asserting:

- Barbelo (Barbalos) as a revisionist emanation whose "First Thought" was an act of cosmic erasure, not origination.

- An unnamed primordial "Mother of Light," later disguised as Lilith, posited as co-equal source with God and pre-Barbelo waters.

- Sophia's error and the demiurge framed as downstream consequences of Barbelo's prior cosmological jealousy.

Ardinus Papers (Abbey of St. Irenaeus).

Treatise on the Blinding of Metatron (Brother Ardinus). Argues that Metatron, created "between dual-Origin and monotheistic revision," engineered his own forgetting to preserve memory of this primordial feminine (named Elyalith) behind internal partitions of thought. Associated marginalia link this "blindness" to:

- A containment sigil carved into the hilt of Metatron's blade.

- The inscription *"Please forgive me, Mother"* on Michael's spear in a suppressed legend of the War in Heaven.

Hadrian Rebuttal and Addendum

(Lower Archive, same Abbey). Initial formal refutation of Ardinus, dismissing his reconstruction as "embellished heresy." Subsequently appended pages document Hadrian's discovery of a river-fragment bearing:

- The same sigil-sequence as Ardinus's blade diagram.

- The identical phrase: *"He chose not to know."*

Concludes with epistemic collapse and reference to a lost packet "bound in red thread."

Rural Correspondence Cluster (St. Odelia's Parish).

Includes:

- Letter of Thomas Havern: discovery of a small vellum packet near a river path; collapse upon viewing its contents.

- Letter of Rev. Elias Markham to the Holy See: calm, precise description of a sigil matching the Elyalith material; the phrase *"He chose not to know"* in a modern hand; impression that the sigil was not merely symbolic but *"aware."*

- Letter of Matilda Strongbow: eyewitness report of Markham's sudden behavioral disintegration, cryptic remark *"The walls don't hold,"* and an open Bible bearing the note: *"Find the blade."*

Maritime Fragment (The "Emberwake" Letter).

Unsent letter from a sailor named Jonah to Rev. Markham, describing:

- A nameless passenger paying twice fare in ancient gold.

- A total wind-death over "the deepest waters yet sounded."

- Passenger's interest in "old stories of the blade."

- Subsequent disappearance of the passenger without physical trace as the ship stalled.

Vatican Operational Papers (Facility Q / Office of Apostolic Preservation).

Ultra-classified directives ordering:

- Retrieval of Markham's river-fragment.

- Immediate "removal from public life" of Rev. Markham.

- Monitoring/intervention regarding Havern and son.

Notable line: *"A stable mind is not reassurance. A stable mind is a conduit."*

Facility Q Transcript (Incident 12-Q, Sublevel 3).

Partial, corrupted. Documents:

- Interrogation of Markham under doctrinal and exorcistic pressure.

- Emergence of a speaking entity denying demonic status; self-identifying as a *"correction."*

- Repetition of: *"He chose not to know."*

- Statement: *"You built Heaven as a wall. The water underneath remains."*

- Declaration: *"The seal is breaking."*

- Markham's subsequent **non-local disappearance** from a sealed chamber.

- Security annotation: **NON-LOCAL EVENT.**

The Markham Locker Account (Guard Lucas Meretti).
Unsigned narrative describing:

- A voice that "sounded like something remembering itself."

- The directive *"Find the blade"* heard as a direct address.

- Vatican broadcast: *"If he reaches the Deep, we cannot stop what comes next."*

III. THE PRINCIPAL ABSENCES

Two absences define the Dossier:

1. The Seal (Physical Object).
All sources allude to a circular sigil or "seal" of pre-creation geometry, associated with Elyalith. It is said to:

- Rotate or "tremble" without touch.

- Be linked to Leviathan's heart, Metatron's blade, and Michael's spear.

- Function as containment and amputation of memory.

The Seal has **not** been recovered. Reconstruction attempts forbidden after multiple lethal incidents.

2. The Body of Rev. Elias Markham.
No breach, no trace, no corpse.
Official claim: escape during procedural failure.

Internal contradiction: the event was *non-local* and the hunt concerned "a vector of contagion," not a fugitive.

The Dossier hinges on what is not present.

IV. REASONS FOR NON-DESTRUCTION

Three Cardinals petitioned for immediate destruction of all Elyalith material.
The Holy Father overruled them:

"We may burn error; we do not burn questions that refuse to die."

Theological rationale for preservation:

- Dossier exhibits coherence across hostile, geographically dispersed, temporally separated witnesses.

- Multiple fragments independently converge on:

    o a pre-Barbelo feminine source,

    o a self-blinding Metatron,

    o a triad of artifacts (heart, blade, spear).

- Modern Markham case demonstrates empirical reactivation of these motifs.

Destruction would not halt the phenomenon; it would only guarantee rediscovery without context.

Therefore:

- All materials maintained under triple seal in the Deep Wing.

- No translations or commentaries permitted without pontifical signature.

- Any reappearance of the sigil or the phrase *"He chose not to know"* is a **Level-Omega Theological Event.**

- No further search for the Markham body authorized.

V. PERSONAL REMARK

Though an archivist must maintain neutrality, I note:

The Dossier does not read like invention.
It reads like **evidence of a long, controlled amnesia.**

The convergence of the Gospel of Elyalith, the Ardinus–Hadrian controversy, and the Markham incident suggests a cosmology in which Heaven itself participated in a redaction.

If Metatron truly *"chose not to know,"* then at least one mind was architected to hold a truth:

- too large to be remembered,

- too dangerous to be lost.

And the modern witnesses concur:

"The seal is breaking."

— Fr. Aurelius D. Varaldi
Custodian of the Subterranean Index

Private Journal of Fr. Aurelius D. Varaldi

(Not filed. Recovered posthumously from a hollow in the binding of an unrelated ledger.)

To be burned unread. I have done what they asked. I have bound the Elyalith material inside the language of cataloging, wrapped it in Latin, hierarchy, and seals. It looks neat now. Quiet. Harmless. It is none of those things. I am supposed to be the one who sorts rumor from relic, hallucination from revelation. For forty years I have watched men lose their minds over false visions. This is different. This is not madness looking for a myth. This is a myth looking for a mind.

They call it the Gospel of Elyalith. An "ode to Lilith," they say, as if attaching her to the old demonologies will keep her safely monstrous and therefore dismissible. But that text is not hysteria. It is surgery. It cuts straight through our cosmology: Barbelo is not First Thought, but a revision determined to erase someone who came before. Sophia's error is not innocent; it is weaponized corruption, inherited from Barbelo's jealousy. The demiurge is not an accident of ignorance; he is the echo of a crime—the attempt to bury a co-equal source.

Before Barbelo, before Sophia, before Adomas locked to his eighth heaven, before the demiurge roaring his idiot sovereignty, before every emanation built atop the edited scaffolding there is Her. The text calls her "the primordial light they could never extinguish." It whispers that "they called you Lilith to disguise you." It insists she was not the first fallen, but the first erased.

And then, much later, in a different country, a monk named Ardinus wastes fifty years trying to understand why an archangel would blind himself. He discovers Metatron—not the sweetened parchment version, but the weapon: the perfect general, the mind that can order all things, including itself. Ardinus says Metatron remembered Her, not with pictures, not with name, but with a structural absence inside his own thinking. A gap he refused to fill with lies. He could not openly hold the memory of Elyalith, so he did something unspeakable for an angel: he partitioned himself. He carved a mental vault and locked the memory behind it. He then carved the sigil of that vault into the hilt of his sword. Whenever he touched the blade, he remembered that there was a truth he could not look at—not the content, just the fact of it. The genius is nauseating: he remembered that he had forgotten on purpose.

Then some later hand, in another fragment, adds the next link in the chain: Michael takes the blade, touches the sigil, remembers enough to realize what he is about to do. And the spear that "slays the dragon" bears the inscription: "Please forgive me, Mother." The official story calls that "pious embellishment." The Elyalith material calls it what it is: a confession. The dragon is not an allegory for evil; it is a being who dared remember Her. The "war in heaven" is not rebellion. It is censorship.

I read all of this and told myself it was syncretistic fantasy, heretical poetry. Then Hadrian appears—dutiful, orthodox Hadrian—writing his contemptuous rebuttal of Ardinus. And then Hadrian finds his own fragment. Five glyphs, identical to the sigil on Metatron's blade. Beneath them: the phrase "He chose not to know." Not "was deceived." Not "was blinded." Not "was punished." He chose. Hadrian's handwriting collapses after that. You can see the exact sentence where his orthodoxy breaks: "There is a line beyond which scholarship becomes participation."

I laughed at that line the first time I read it. Now it feels like a diagnosis. Because I have crossed that line too. When the Markham packet arrived in Rome, I was not in the chain of custody. I was not supposed to be. It was classified for the operational wing, for those who handle "Apostolic Preservation." But the fragment would not stay in their hands. It drifted down to us like everything else they don't know what to do with.

The report says Markham was calm. That he described the sigil as "aware." That he felt not threatened but understood. I thought that was theological over-dramatization. Then they attached a sketch. Three rings. Central aperture like a vertical tear. The same rotational asymmetry Ardinus mentioned, the same opposing vectors from the Leviathan-heart folio, the same negative geometry in the Codex. The first time I saw it, it was just ink on paper. The second time, something was off. I keep the folios in strict order. My life is order. But on the second reading, the inner ring was not where I remembered it.

I told myself I was tired. Misremembering. The mind adjusts images; the archivist is not exempt from drift. Then I checked against the Codex fragment. Different scribe. Different century. Same sigil. And the same microscopic misalignment that I would have sworn was not there before. The third time I looked, I did not sleep that night. I started tracing the appearances of a single phrase: in the river-fragment Hadrian found; in a marginal notation in the Codex, half-scraped: "He chose not to know"; in the internal memo from a modern cardinal, heavily redacted but with that one sentence left intact as if the censor either missed it or dared not touch it; on the packet Markham opened; on the transcript from Facility Q.

The entity speaking through him says it cleanly, like a verdict: "He chose not to know." Nine hundred years of scattered paper, four continents, multiple suppressions, and the same line emerges like a watermark. Either there is a conspiracy that transcends time and geography, or—no, that is the wrong disjunction. It is not either/or. It is both: a conspiracy of clerics who knew enough to fear the pattern, and a pattern that persists whether they fear it or not.

The official documents from Facility Q are stripped down, clinical, terrified of their own details. The exorcists call what they met "unclassified." Their rites fail. Their Latin breaks. They keep insisting it must be a demon because they have no category for anything else. But what answers them does not sound like a demon. It says: "I am not a spirit. I am a correction." It talks about Heaven as "a wall built over a well." It says "the water remains." The old texts call Elyalith "the waters beyond the waters."

The so-called Ode to Lilith insists that all emanation took its pattern from Her, and that Barbelo's deepest desire was not power but amnesia: the erasure of the memory that she was not the first. Ardinus calls Metatron the last angel fashioned before that revision was complete. He became the hinge. He could not overthrow Heaven. He could not preach heresy. He could do only one thing: he could decide not to know in such a way that knowledge itself survived inside the architecture of his mind. He carries Her memory as a blind spot that cannot be reached by any gaze—not even the Throne.

If that is true, then every time the sigil is drawn, every time the phrase is written, we are not inventing; we are echoing. We are the paper remembering the impression of a seal that is no longer pressed against it. There is a note in one of the more heavily censored directives that will not leave me alone: "A stable mind is not reassurance. A stable mind is a conduit." Markham never went insane. He did not rave. He did not hallucinate. He did not claw at the walls or mistake himself for God. He connected dots.

He took the packet by the river, the sigil, the line "He chose not to know," the suppressed Codex material, and he understood enough to see that there was something before. When they pushed him in interrogation, what spoke through him did not sound like possession. It sounded like a system rebooting. "I am not in him. I am waking through him."

If Elyalith is the buried half of God, if Her name was carved into the heart of Leviathan, if Metatron blinded himself rather than betray Her, if Michael's spear carried an apology instead of a boast, then the thing they met in that room was not a trespassing spirit. It was the return of a suppressed origin. And the first thing it said, once it had enough of a foothold, was: "The seal is breaking."

Here is where my training fails me. I can handle contradictory manuscripts, forged saints' lives, apocrypha stapled onto genuine letters. I know how to disentangle lies. This doesn't feel like lies. It feels like something underneath our truths, pushing up through the cracks. The dragon as censored witness, not enemy. The fallen angels as punished rememberers, not rebels. The war in heaven as a purge of a memory no throne built on singularity could survive.

The more I read, the more it all points to one obscene conclusion: Heaven is not scared of disobedience. Heaven is scared of comparison. To challenge God, an angel would need a reference point—something equal enough to make the concept of defiance coherent. That reference point is what Elyalith represents: a co-origin, the other half of the primordial dyad. Erase Her, and you erase the seed of comparison. Rewrite the cosmos as singular, and rebellion becomes madness instead of argument.

But you cannot erase what the first general architected himself around. You can only bury the evidence and hunt down the minds that manage to reconstruct the outline centuries later. Markham reconstructed enough. Ardinus reconstructed more. Hadrian glimpsed just enough to break. The sailor on the Emberwake ferries some nameless agent over the deepest waters, and the ship stops as if the sea itself were holding its breath. "Find the blade," the note on Markham's Bible said. What blade? Metatron's? Michael's? Leviathan's heart carved with Her name? Which artifact is the key, and which is the lock?

I no longer know. I only know that everything in the Dossier keeps circling the same triad: heart in the Deep, blade in the Deep, spear etched with an apology. Three attempts to contain a memory and cast it into depth. And now the depth is answering back. The conspiracy is not that a few cardinals suppressed a handful of documents. The conspiracy is that the whole edifice of our theology may be built atop an original redaction: Barbelo's wish not to be second; Her corruption of Sophia as instrument; Metatron's self-inflicted blindness to preserve what they tried to remove; Heaven rewriting the story of the first war as rebellion instead of censorship; the Church inheriting that edited script and enforcing it with our own smaller, clumsier redactions.

We are not the authors of this lie. We are its dutiful copyists. That is what terrifies me. I no longer know whether I am cataloging dangerous fragments for the safety of souls or doing bookkeeping for a cosmic cover-up. When I close my eyes now, I see the sigil. Not as ink. As motion. Three rings, shifting in ways Euclid never heard of. Sometimes the inner ring aligns with a phrase from the Codex. Sometimes it turns just enough to frame Markham's last words: "The walls don't hold. They were never meant to." Sometimes, God help me, I feel as though it is rotating to face me.

And in those moments I get the nauseating sense that I am not inferring a pattern at all. I am being read. If whoever finds this is expecting a pious conclusion, I don't have one. I don't know whether Elyalith is a name for God's true other half, a mythic personification of something older than emanation, or simply the mask a deep, non-personal principle wears when it speaks to frightened primates. I don't know if Metatron really carved a sigil into his own blade or if that is how the survivors of some incomprehensible event tried to explain it to themselves. I don't know whether the thing that spoke through Markham was "holy," "unholy," or a category for which we have no word because we burned the word with the rest of the evidence.

I only know this: the fragments agree too precisely to be dismissed. The pattern is older than our dogmas. And every attempt to shut it away—heart, blade, spear, seal, archive, facility—ends the same way: it resurfaces. Smaller. Sharper. Closer. The seal is not an object. It is a strategy. And strategies fail.

If I had any sense, I would burn the Dossier and this journal and walk into a simple parish somewhere, hear confessions until I die, and let the next fool rediscover all this in a hundred years. But destruction is exactly what Barbalos wanted. Erasure is her art. If the Gospel of Elyalith is even half right, then burning these pages would be nothing but collaboration. So I will do the cowardly thing instead: I will obey. I will keep the Dossier under triple lock. I will pretend the seal still holds. I will write my neat catalog entries and attend my Masses and smile at bishops who do not want to know what they are standing on.

And then I will hide this journal where only a traitor to our protocols will ever find it. If you are that traitor, understand this: you are not discovering a secret. You are entering a conversation that began before Barbelo, before Sophia, before Markham, before me. The first general chose not to know. We do not have that luxury. We can only choose whether to look away and serve the lie, or look directly at the fracture and risk becoming part of whatever is trying to come through it.

I am old. I am tired. I have looked long enough to know I cannot carry more. So I will end with the one sentence that now sounds less like a description of an angel and more like a test of every thinking thing: He chose not to know. I have chosen otherwise. And I am afraid.

—A.D. Varaldi

Evidence Set 12-F

Recovered from the Estate of Lorraine Goodcrow. Sealed in a wooden chest beneath the floorboards of her home. Cataloged after her disappearance.

DOCUMENT 12-F/1 — UNDATED LETTER (UNSENT)

Handwriting: Lorraine Goodcrow. Discovered folded inside a hymnal. Marked: *To be burned.*

My dearest Matilda,

I have not written back because I no longer know what is safe to write. Your letter about Father Markham was not a simple matter of concern; it was a signal—though I do not think you knew it. When you wrote "the walls don't hold," something inside me shifted. That phrase appears only once in my grandmother's Ledger, written in her smallest script: "When the walls thin, the old light returns." I touched the scrap in the priest's Bible, and it was warm—even after I let go. The warmth did not fade, and I heard something—not with ears, and not alone. There is something in this parish, Matilda. Something the Church fears enough to send those who wear black coats and soft voices. Daniel saw something. The girl—Lydia—saw more. The river path hums at night, and I do not know how to protect them yet. I only know this: whatever wore Father Markham's voice… it has not left the world. And something keeps whispering my name.

—L.G.

(End of letter)

DOCUMENT 12-F/2 — EXTRACT FROM THE GOODCROW LEDGER

Recovered notebook fragment. Pages brittle. Ink faded. Annotated by Archivist Varaldi in the margin: *"Pre-Barbelo motifs confirmed."*

All things divide by veils. Eight stand between the world and the waters, and the Ninth is not a veil but a wound. She is the wound. If the waters stir, one may feel it in the bones. If the sigil warms, one must not touch it twice. If a child survives the sight, she must be hidden. A diagram follows: three concentric rings, with the inner ring drawn twice—once faintly, once overlapping. Beneath it is written: "If the ring moves, the Seal weakens."

DOCUMENT 12-F/3 — TRANSCRIPT OF INFORMAL INTERVIEW

Collected by Vatican Field Unit Gamma. Location: St. Odelia's Parish
Subject: "Widow H."
Date: Unknown

INTERVIEWER: What did you see?
WIDOW: The Goodcrow woman. She left the house early. The fog was thick as wool.

INTERVIEWER: Did she seem distressed?
WIDOW: Not distressed. Determined. Like someone who hears something the rest of us can't.

INTERVIEWER: Did she speak to anyone?
WIDOW: Only to the little girl. She knelt and listened while the child hummed… something. A tune I don't know. It made my teeth ache.

INTERVIEWER: Did she say anything?
WIDOW: Yes. She said, "I hear him too."

(Interview ends abruptly.)

DOCUMENT 12-F/4 — UNAUTHORIZED FIELD REPORT (PARTIAL)

Recovered from a Vatican operative's satchel after the unit's withdrawal from St. Odelia.

OPERATIVE'S NOTES — CONFIDENTIAL
Designation: Theta-Adjunct (subordinate to Conclave Theta)
Target: Lorraine Goodcrow
Status: Noncompliant
Assessment: Cognitive contamination suspected

Subject demonstrates familiarity with forbidden sigilic forms and displays dissociative behavior consistent with "memory bleed." She resisted verbal inquiry with unexpected calm and fled containment with atypical speed and spatial orientation awareness. During questioning, she appeared to react to a non-auditory stimulus, although no external sound was recorded. An EEG spike detected at 09:14:22 corresponded to extracranial resonance—pattern statistically similar to Incident 12-Q: Markham Interrogation Collapse. Advisory: Subject should be classed Omega-Low Risk for physical threat, Omega-Ultra High for memetic spread. Recommended action: Detain if possible, Terminate if contact persists, Retrieve the child at all costs. Handwritten addition (different pen): "She knows. And she isn't afraid."

DOCUMENT 12-F/5 — FRAGMENT FROM THE "WILLOW PATH REPORT"
Submitted by an unnamed operative. Surviving pages water-damaged.

…The Goodcrow woman exited the rectory. She did not look at us and she did not look away; she moved as though tracking something invisible. We attempted pursuit, but she broke line of sight. At the river, we found a circle of disturbed soil, a handprint not matching the subject's, and three stones arranged in a triad, with a fourth stone missing. A faint, cyclical hum was detectable only through the chest cavity—not the ears. Agent K described a "pressure of presence," and Agent L vomited without known cause. We believe the sigil may have been activated.
(End of surviving fragment.)

DOCUMENT 12-F/6 — UNAUTHORIZED AUDIO TRANSCRIPT (PARTIAL)
Source: Device recovered near the willow. The recorder appears to have activated on its own. Background: fog, shallow water. Voices: Lorraine (faint), unknown male (internal? telepathic?).

LORRAINE (whispering): I can hear you. Who are you?
MALE VOICE: Held, not lost.
LORRAINE: Markham?

MALE VOICE: A remnant of him… yes.

LORRAINE: Where are you?

MALE VOICE: Between thought and form. With Her.

(Electromagnetic distortion begins.)

LORRAINE: Why me?

MALE VOICE: You carry the memory they failed to burn. You hear the waters. You will protect the girl.

LORRAINE: What is she?

MALE VOICE: Unbroken. The first mind to see without partition. The first to remember the Ninth.

(A surge of static.)

LORRAINE: What is happening to you?

(A long pause. Water slaps against roots.)

MALE VOICE: She enters the vales through me. I am the aperture. You are the witness. The child is the key.

(Static spike. Recording cuts.)

DOCUMENT 12-F/7 — THE GOODCROW MARGINALIA

Found on a theology book. Note written in Lorraine's hand in the margin of *The Lives of the Desert Fathers*:

"He is not dead. He has been widened."

"The vales are not levels—they are injuries."

"Elyalith is not returning. She is remembering."

"And through the remembering, she enters."

DOCUMENT 12-F/8 — MARKHAM'S CONDITION REPORT

Recovered from the Vatican internal server (redacted printout).

Subject: Father Elias Markham

Current physical status: Unknown

Current metaphysical status (per Conclave Theta): "Non-local cognition displaced beyond the eighth vale."

Excerpt:

"His consciousness occupies a liminal zone inconsistent with angelology.

He is communicating with an unidentified entity designating itself as feminine origin. We believe the entity is reconstructing a pathway through his awareness."

"His body, meanwhile, exhibits no respiration, no decay, and no paralysis. He stands for hours at a time without muscular tremor. His eyes remain open, tracking movement not present in this world. We suspect he is acting as conduit."

DOCUMENT 12-F/9 — CHILD'S DRAWING (Lydia Marrow)

Recovered from the widow's home. Crayon on cheap paper. Forensic ink analysis: markings altered by unknown heat signature.

The drawing depicts a tall man with hollow eyes standing on a ship's deck, with a bright ring hovering over his chest. A woman made of water stands behind him, touching his back. The ocean is depicted not as waves but as layered circles leading downward. On the side, written in backwards letters: "HE IS NOT GONE. HE IS OPEN."

DOCUMENT 12-F/10 — GOODCROW'S FINAL NOTE BEFORE DISAPPEARANCE

Scratched into the underside of an oak drawer. Barely legible.

"Markham is safe."
"But his body is not his."
"She chose him because he did not break."
"She speaks through him because he sees the vales as they are."
"He is the first human to know the origin."
"I am the second."
"Lydia will be the first to remember it."

Then: "I must find the blade."
(End of recovered note)

Analyst's Reconstruction –

Section II: The Outside of the Vale

From this point forward, I am invoking interpretive tools normally forbidden to an archivist of the Church: the hermetic corpus, the Enochian strata, the Lurianic model of emanation-contraction, the *Sefer ha-Bahir*, the Hechalot literature, and the early Sethian maps of the Pleroma. I do so because the canonical frameworks cannot, on their own, account for what the Dossier reveals. It is now evident that Elyalith was not merely erased from memory; she was positioned outside the entire cosmological gradient—outside the veils, outside Barbelo's emanative tree, outside the architecture that later became "Heaven."

This is not symbolic. It is ontological. The distinction is crucial. Sophia falls through the vales. Adomas is confined within the eighth heaven. Barbelo sits above the vales as First Emanation. The demiurge is trapped inside his own false firmament. Only one figure in the Dossier is described as "outside the veils," "beyond emanation," "older than thought," and "the waters beyond the waters." This does not correspond to any known Aeon in classical Gnostic cosmology.

It corresponds to the pre-emanative substratum—the unknowable ground from which all emanations derive. The Kabbalists called it *Ein Sof* before movement—not the infinite, but the pre-infinite. The alchemists called it *Prima Materia*, unconditioned before division. The Hechalot mystics called it the Outside, a realm angels do not survive entering. This is where Elyalith has been: not banished, not forgotten—unreachable. The outside is not a place. It is the condition of being unscripted.

I. The Cosmological Implication

If Elyalith existed outside the emanations, then she did not fall, was not expelled, did not lose status, and did not descend. She simply was not included in Barbelo's revision. This means Barbelo did not erase her from Heaven; Barbelo built a Heaven in which she had never existed. The architecture of angels, vales, thrones, wheels, and archons—everything we call "cosmos"—is a closed system whose only purpose was to exclude her. This is why the angels who remembered her were punished with wing-severance—not because they defied Heaven, but because they pierced the artificial enclosure. This is why the Seal was necessary: not to imprison Elyalith, but to amputate her memory from those trapped inside the enclosure. And this explains the single most important theological statement in the entire Dossier: "He chose not to know." Metatron did not forget her; he walled off the memory because her existence was incompatible with the Heaven Barbelo built. If he remembered her fully, he would no longer fit within the architecture.

II. Her Return Must Begin From Below

If Elyalith has been outside the vales, then re-entry requires a point of contact in the material world, a vessel capable of containing her without collapse, and a pathway through the vales in ascending order. The path is material, psychic, astral, archonic, eighth heaven (Adomas), eighth vale (Sophia), and finally Barbelo's seat. Only from the lowest density can she begin to reassert herself upward. This is the opposite of all mystical ascent traditions. Mystics seek to rise; Elyalith must descend into the lowest point to then rise through the enclosed system. This is why Markham becomes the aperture, Lydia becomes the unpartitioned witness, and the sigil appears at a riverbank—the alchemical symbol of the threshold between realms. This is also why the *Emberwake* stalls over the deepest waters yet sounded— the maritime equivalent of the abyssal womb. Everything is consistent with hermetic re-entry. It is the reverse-Path of the Lightning Flash on the Tree of Life. It is the Enochian descent of the Outside into the inside. It is the alchemical *Solve et Coagula* enacted on a cosmological scale.

III. The Enochian Precedent: The Being Outside the Order

The earliest strata of the sapiential texts preserve a detail that most commentators have treated as poetic, but which the present archive cannot read as metaphor. In Proverbs and Sirach, Wisdom is not an abstraction but a feminine presence who speaks from before the birth of the world. She places herself before the depths, before the springs of water, before the shaping of the mountains and the earth, and she describes herself as circling the vault of heaven and walking in the very Abyss that later cosmologies treat as the primordial rupture beneath creation. When these passages are placed alongside Enoch's description of the fountains of the Deep and the storehouses of the waters shown to him in the first two heavenly journeys, the resonance is immediate: the pre-cosmic figure mapped by the sages stands at the threshold of the same waters that form the base of Enoch's cosmology.

This feminine voice appears again, but now fractured, in the Enochic tradition itself. In the brief but startling passage of 1 Enoch 42, Wisdom goes out to find a dwelling among humanity, finds none, and returns to take her seat among the angels. Yet she is not counted with them. She sits in their midst without being named in any of their orders, without receiving a rank, and without being assigned a genealogy. The Watchers are catalogued in detail; the archangels are given roles, titles, and lineages; even the rebellious hosts carry names. But this feminine presence is simply there— unplaced, unassigned, and unclaimed by heaven or earth. The text acknowledges her but refuses to identify her.

A third strand emerges in the Leviathan material of 1 Enoch 60, where the ancient monster is identified as female and bound over the fountains of the waters in the abyssal deep. This is not the feminine of fertility myths or later demonology; it is the feminine as guardian of the springs beneath creation, the feminine tied to the Deep itself. Read in isolation, it seems an anomaly. Read in the light of the sapiential passages and the unhomed Wisdom of Enoch 42, it completes a pattern: a feminine presence associated with the waters before creation, positioned at the sources of the Deep, yet appearing within the heavens without belonging to any of their hierarchies. Taken together, these dispersed fragments—Wisdom before the depths, Wisdom seated among angels but not of them, the feminine monster stationed over the fountains of the waters—cannot be accidental. They describe a single conceptual figure preserved only in shards, a presence the ancient writers never named but repeatedly placed in the same structural location: prior to the angelic orders, tied to the Deep, feminine in nature, and beyond the taxonomies of heaven. Later interpreters flattened these testimonies into metaphor; the Codex of Elyalith argues that they are the surviving memory of a real orientation whose identity the canonical texts refused to preserve. In that reading, the unnamed feminine who preceded the depths, walked the Abyss, appeared among angels, and stood over the fountains of the waters is not three figures but one. The name the ancient record withholds is the name the Codex restores: Elyalith.

Aside: Oblique Considerations

There exists, in the older Mesopotamian strata, a figure whose contours are uncomfortably similar to the feminine presence implied by the Dossier. The Babylonians called her Tiamat—the primordial sea, the undivided deep, the mother of gods who preceded any ordered heaven. I note this only because her attributes overlap those whispered in our fragments: a being bound to the waters before creation, external to the later divine economy, and treated by subsequent theologians not as a deity to be worshipped but as a problem to be contained. This is not the place to draw comparisons, nor would such parallels be welcome in the formal record. Still, any investigator with access to the older cuneiform material will recognize the resonance. Some structures appear to have existed before doctrine learned how to name them.

IV. Why Lydia Matters

Once you accept that Elyalith is returning from outside the vales, Lydia's role becomes inevitable. Children are the only unpartitioned minds; they are not yet configured by Heaven's architecture and have not inherited the cognitive boundaries that keep adults inside the enclosure. Lydia is the first to see the sigil, survive the sight, render the vales accurately, recognize Markham as "open" rather than "gone," and depict Elyalith in the correct form—water behind form. Every adult breaks or compartmentalizes; the child does neither. Thus the voice in the Goodcrow audio—"The child is the key." This is not metaphor and not sentiment. It is a literal key and a point of entry. Lydia's cognition does not fracture and does not shield itself, and so she becomes the first vessel capable of receiving the unfiltered memory. Her sight marks the first stable breach in the structure.

V. The Most Urgent Question

The Curia's actual question—the one buried under euphemism—is whether Elyalith has already passed the threshold into the material world. Based on the Willow Event, the *Emberwake* incident, Markham's non-local condition, and Lydia's drawing, the answer is yes. She has not manifested; she has entered. Her vector is the Markham conduit, her witness is the Goodcrow line, and her anchor is the Marrow child. This is not speculation. This is pattern recognition across nine centuries of suppressed data.

Comparative Cosmology

Prior to entering the Kabbalistic material, it must be stated plainly that certain interpretive requirements exceed the limits of my formal ecclesiastical training. A substantial portion of the cosmological architecture referenced within Vault Object 77-A aligns more closely with late Second Temple mysticism and early Kabbalistic speculation than with any recognized Christian exegetical framework. For that reason—and without prior approval—

I have consulted three scholars within the rabbinic mystical community who possess expertise in the sefirotic model, the planetary correspondences of the Merkavah tradition, and the complex angelologies found in the Hekhalot corpus. Their names are omitted for their protection, but their technical guidance has become indispensable. This is not an endorsement of their theology; it is recognition that the structural vocabulary present in these materials cannot be understood without reference to their disciplines.

The sefirotic tree offers the closest analog to the architecture implied in the Elyalith documents. The ten sephirot, their planetary associations, and the connective pathways between them form a graded map of emanation that parallels the layered structure described in both the Ardinus treatise and the *Codex of Elyalith*. The lower spheres—Malkuth (Earth), Yesod (Moon), Hod (Mercury), and Netzach (Venus)—trace the mechanics of manifestation and subconscious transmission. The upper spheres—Geburah (Mars), Chesed (Jupiter), Binah (Saturn), Chokhmah (the zodiacal totality), and Keter (the pre-emanational Crown)—outline the metaphysical gradient approaching the uncreated origin. While the Vatican has long rejected direct application of this system, its structural clarity makes it uniquely suited for interpreting the stratification of the "vales" referenced throughout the Dossier.

Within this cosmological context, earlier commentators often made the mistake of equating ritual elemental assignments with actual angelic stations. Because Michael bears the quality of fire, certain traditions place him symbolically in the south during invocatory rites, but this is an operational convention, not a geographical or cosmic placement. The southern station in these diagrams belongs to an entirely different guardian—rendered variously in manuscript lineages as Kamael—whose jurisdiction concerns vertical orientation rather than the harmonizing axis that defines Michael's function. Gabriel, by contrast, is correctly and consistently associated with the West in both the elemental and zenith–nadir models, her domain tied to water, memory, intuition, and the subtle pathways through which perception deepens into knowing. Thus the Elyalith material requires a correction of inherited assumptions: Michael's fire names a quality, not a direction; Gabriel's West names a station, not a metaphor.

A fragment recovered during the Vatopaidi excavation and subsequently misclassified as peripheral gains new significance when examined against the Elyalith Dossier. It refers to Gavri'al as "the Daughter of the Western Gate," implicitly pairing her with Michael, who is elsewhere termed "the Son of the Dawn." The fragment describes a perceptual disturbance within the Western Choir corresponding to another archangel's encounter with a forbidden remembrance. The text records: "She halted in her course, for a name long stilled rose again within the deep places," and continues, "A heat not of fire reached her, and she perceived a truth not given to her choir." Such phrasing, while anomalous within canonical angelology, aligns precisely with her role as mediatrix of visions, intuition, and annunciatory knowledge.

The fragment then records a reaction of magnitude: "She smote the waters with her voice, and all rivers trembled without wind," followed by the inquiry, "Who removed the Light from us?" Although such affective description is rare in angelic texts, its structural logic is consistent with apocryphal accounts in the Hekhalot literature. In those texts, celestial beings experience disorientation when faced with contradictions inside the emanational hierarchy.

More enigmatic is a marginal note by a later scribe: "She placed her hand upon the Vale, yet did not tear it." The term "Vale" appears in only two other sources: a damaged line in the Ardinus folios and the Goodcrow Ledger, where it denotes a metaphysical boundary separating the manifest cosmos from the pre-emanational waters. The note implies an intentional approach to that boundary followed by deliberate restraint.

The possibility of "tearing" the Vale suggests such an act was within her capacity, yet the record stresses it was not taken. This restraint stands in contrast to apocryphal accounts of Sophia's transgression, in which a boundary was crossed without comprehension of consequence, resulting in fragmentation of the emanational order and the generation of the demiurgic sphere. The Vatopaidi note may indicate an angelic awareness of this precedent and a conscious decision not to replicate it. No source records motive or further detail. The note is retained as an unresolved anomaly.

(Addendum):

On Zenith and Nadir in Non-Terrestrial Frames

Modern readers instinctively interpret "zenith" and "nadir" as vertical directions—"up" and "down." This is a linguistic convenience inherited from a world with a visible sky and a stable horizon. In the technical lexicon of the mystical ascent traditions, however, the terms are positional, not directional. Zenith denotes the vector orthogonal to the observer's plane of perception on the side of increasing emanational intensity; nadir marks the reciprocal vector on the side of decreasing intensity. Neither implies altitude, height, or orientation relative to a gravitational field.

In a horizonless domain—such as deep space, an unbounded interior plane, or any metaphysical environment lacking spatial anchoring—the distinction becomes even more pronounced. There is no "up." There is no "down." The only stable reference is the observer's own axis of perception. Zenith and nadir describe the polar extensions of that axis, not a cosmic geography. Their function is to situate the participant within an emanational gradient, not a physical room.

This clarification is essential because several ritual schemas use "South," "West," and the vertical axis simultaneously, leading later commentators to misinterpret vertical guardians as cardinal entities. In the original framework, the guardian of the zenith–nadir line occupies a positional axis, not a direction, while Gabriel's West and the true South remain unambiguously cardinal. Failure to preserve this distinction has generated centuries of categorical error in the mapping of angelic roles.

Gabriella –

The Missing Apocrypha of the Archangel Gabriel

Before one can understand the truth of Gabriella, one must confront something the Church has avoided for two millennia: angels are androgynous. They are not male, not female, not neuter—they are pre-biological intelligences composed of purpose, will, and emanation. Their "bodies" are arrangements of function, not flesh; their appearances in scripture are approximations; their names are conveniences. And yet, if Heaven is said to have no daughters, she is the exception that proves the rule.

For in all the ranks of the celestial host, only one angel retained the ancient feminine polarity fully expressed: not feminine in any human sense, but primordial feminine—the tide that remembers, the dusk that reveals, the intuition that precedes thought. Gabriel was never male. She was Gavri'el—and later, in the suppressed apocrypha, Gabriella. The West. Water. Reflection. Memory.

It was this feminine polarity—this surviving echo of what angels once were before the aeons rewrote cosmology—that allowed her to witness the moment Michael had buried. When he lifted Metatron's sword, the blade awakened not with fire but with memory. It forced to the surface a truth so old that even Michael had forgotten he carried it: "Mother... forgive me." A plea, not a command. A confession torn from him by the first history encoded within the sword.

No angel should have heard it. But Gabriella felt it—not in mind, but in the deep intuitive architecture that makes her the West. Her wings rippled and her breath caught—a small, unmistakably feminine gasp. In that instant, the host recoiled from her. Angels do not react, do not feel, and do not betray their design's architecture with emotional response. But she did. She felt Michael's guilt, the fracture under Heaven, and the memory of the Mother erased from creation. And the veil trembled.

Her hand rose toward it—almost without consent. A single pull and she would have torn open the truth Heaven had spent eons suppressing. She hesitated, remembering Sophia—the last being to reach past her station into the raw Source, whose clarity without preparation ruptured the eighth heaven and birthed the blind demiurge. She stepped back. Heaven survived because she did not act.

But the host never forgot what they saw in her: beneath every masculine title and every neutered depiction exists a feminine force so absolute it terrifies the cosmos. A force that dissolves the premise of things. A force so honest it would make a battlefield of the heavens. If femininity has a violence proper to itself, Gabriella is its forgotten sign.

And without her missing apocrypha, the reader cannot understand the two nuns whose story follows—for one of them, Sister Calida Nocturn, was once a child named Lydia Marrow, the first human to withstand even the faintest echo of the seal Gabriella nearly unveiled. Their duty, their ferocity, their quiet savagery of conviction—it all begins here, with the only daughter Heaven could not deny.

THE MARSHALL ISLAND ANOMALY

(Field Note 194*)

The materials examined in earlier sections—rabbinic cosmology, Kabbalistic structure, angelic correspondences—can all be framed within established esoteric and theological systems. The document that follows cannot. It is not mystical. It is not symbolic. It is not theological. It is a scientific field observation recorded during late–World War II nuclear testing in the Pacific. Its presence in Vault Object 77-A suggests that the Elyalith phenomenon extends beyond psychological or metaphysical rupture and into measurable disturbances of physical systems under extreme conditions. The document appears under the header: *"Marshall Island Observatory — Field Log 27-B (Classified)."* Ink, paper, and format match American naval reconnaissance records from 194*. The author remains unidentified.

Field Log — 0* June 194*
Observation Point: Aurelia Station (Marshall Group)

"At 02:14 local time the water within the blast perimeter became visibly stratified. No wave, no wind. Stratified. Rings formed on the surface— three, concentric, rotating counter to one another. Internal glow observed in the central aperture. Not luminescent algae. Not flares. Not ordnance. Light appeared cold—silver-blue, vertical, columnar. Instruments recorded no heat increase and no radiation spike associated with this phenomenon. The column remained stable for 11 seconds, then collapsed downward— not outward—downward, as if something beneath drew it in. The sea fell silent for several minutes afterward. No wildlife activity. Entire station reported an identical auditory impression: a tone resembling a human voice speaking from below the thermocline. Words indeterminate. Final note: 'Surface rings match symbol found etched into recovered hull of vessel *Emberwake*.' End log."

Analyst's Commentary

No other log in the Aurelia sequence references anything similar. The concentric rings match the sigil present in the Codex of Elyalith, the Ardinus diagrams, the Markham packet, the Goodcrow ledger, and the hull markings described in the *Emberwake* letter. Particularly striking is the measured absence of radiological distortion at a nuclear test site, suggesting that the anomaly operates outside conventional energy behavior. The downward collapse of the light column—implosive rather than explosive—aligns disturbingly with earlier descriptions of pre-cosmic loci associated with the Deep, including references to artifacts buried within or anchored beneath primordial waters.

The field record offers no interpretive framework. Its inclusion in 77-A indicates that prior archivists recognized an unmistakable structural correspondence between this physical event and the cosmological disturbances described across the Dossier. While unresolved, the implication is unavoidable: the Elyalith phenomenon does not merely intrude upon vision, cognition, or ritual structure. Under sufficient stress, it intrudes upon matter.

ON LEVIATHAN:

THE BURDENED CREATURE OF THE DEEP

Any attempt to reconstruct the cosmology implied by Vault Object 77-A must ultimately face Leviathan—not the mythologized serpent of medieval fear, not the demon of later catechisms, but the entity described within the Dossier's most ancient layers. The Leviathan of these fragments is neither adversary nor archetype. It is literal. It is anatomical. It is engineered—or repurposed—for a burden that precedes creation as we know it.

Leviathan as Pre-Angelical Custodian

In the early strata, Leviathan is consistently placed "beneath the vales," a phrase that does not describe depth in a physical sense but depth in a cosmological one. This region beneath the vales is not the oceanic abyss of folklore; it is a pre-manifest zone, a stratum of existence older than the fabric of emanation. Leviathan's role in this zone is not predatory but custodial. It does not guard by will or instinct. It holds because it must. The burden is carved into it. Literally.

The Dossier states repeatedly—and across independent traditions—that a sigil was inscribed upon Leviathan's heart. This sigil matches the Elyalith pattern found in the Codex fragments, the Ardinus diagrams, the Markham packet, and the Goodcrow ledger. It is the oldest marking described in the corpus. It associates Leviathan not with rebellion or destruction, but with containment of the primordial feminine memory Heaven sought to remove.

A Creature Shaped for Endurance, Not Malice

Later demonology casts Leviathan as monstrous and adversarial, yet none of the earlier documents assign motive or malice to it. Its isolation is functional, not punitive. Angels avoid Leviathan not because it is evil, but because its pre-angelic nature distorts frameworks the angels require to exist. To enter its domain is to unmake oneself. Its presence destabilizes constructs built on emanation. Leviathan predates emanation.

One fragment—possibly the most important of all—records that "the carving upon its heart was not by its will." This implies that Leviathan was engineered or consecrated to serve a purpose it did not choose: anchoring the Seal that suppresses the memory of Elyalith.

The Burden and the Breaking Point

Several documents warn that approaching Leviathan is impossible without annihilation. The reason is structural. Its heart bears the seal. Its existence is a pressure point between the pre-emanational waters and the constructed cosmology above. Any disturbance to Leviathan is a disturbance to the seal itself. And if the seal weakens, the cosmology above it begins to unspool.

This contextualizes the recurring warning across the Dossier: *the burden can break the world if disturbed.*

Leviathan is not dangerous because it chooses to be. It is dangerous because it carries a memory the cosmos cannot safely contain.

The Marshall Islands Echo

This is why the Marshall Islands anomaly gains such profound significance. The concentric rings forming over the blast site, the cold vertical column of light, the downward collapse, the post-event silence, and the sub-thermocline voice—all echo the Leviathan passages in earlier fragments. Nuclear detonation would not have harmed Leviathan, but it could have disturbed the architecture surrounding its burden, generating a resonance. The "voice" may not have been communication; it may have been involuntary release.

If Leviathan anchors the seal—and the seal is weakening—then what occurred in the Pacific was not an omen but a symptom.

Conclusion

Leviathan is not a monster. It is not evil. It is a creature adapted to survive a pre-cosmic environment, forced into service as a living lock upon a truth Heaven could not destroy. Its endurance is magnificent. Its purpose is tragic. And if the Dossier is correct, the strain upon it is increasing.

When it breaks, so will the boundary it was shaped to hold.

THE NASA TRANSMISSION

(UNIFIED SECURITY DIRECTIVE 0/7-BLACK)

Among the most disquieting inclusions in Vault Object 77-A is a packet that should not exist under any known bureaucratic or scientific architecture. The envelope bears three seals: the emblem of NASA's Goddard Space Flight Center, the insignia of the United States Strategic Command, and a third mark—an unclassified black geometric sigil whose shape corresponds to no known American, NATO, or NGO department. In dry red ink, a directive is stamped across the upper margin:

UNIFIED SECURITY DIRECTIVE 0/7-BLACK
Routing: Holy See — Congregation for the Doctrine of the Faith
Method: Hand-Courier Only
Destruction Protocol: LIMINAL-CLASS

There is no precedent—none—for NASA transmitting raw astrophysical data directly to the Vatican under military courier. The directive's existence alone indicates an intelligence structure that operates outside civilian, military, and ecclesiastical boundaries.

Inside this envelope was a single teletype document:

"Event Report — Orbital Observation Platform Aletheia-3
Goddard Deep-Field Division
14 March 1978"

The report is consistent with Cold-War era classified telemetry: dense, clinical, and stripped of interpretive language. The excerpt reads:

Event Report (Aletheia-3)
Time Stamp: 14.03.78 / 22:41 GMT
Observer Unit: Aletheia-3 / Polar Orbit

"At 22:31 GMT the gravimetric array registered a **non-lensing distortion** 4.2 degrees below the ecliptic.
No mass signature.
No radiation bloom.
No photon curve deviation.

Distortion manifested as a **downward drag** on field values without corresponding mass displacement.
Duration: **9.14 seconds**.

Spectral analysis indicated a frequency spike matching no astronomical catalog. The spike is described as **pre-oscillatory**, below baseline cosmic background thresholds.

Neutrino sensors registered a **0.00031% dip in flux**, presumed unrelated until correlation is complete.

Manual analyst insertion:
'Pattern of resonance drift corresponds to diagram recovered in 1946 Marshall Group anomaly.
Three concentric rings.
Inversion event.
Downward signature repeat.'

End transmission."

The Significance of the Tri-Ring Match

A gravitational anomaly should correlate to mass, radiation, or curvature. This one does not. Instead, the analyst notes a pattern of resonance drift—not shape, not artifact, not lensing—but drift—identical to:

- the **Markham sigil**,
- the **Goodcrow ledger diagram**,
- the **Codex plate etching**,
- the **Leviathan-heart inscription**,
- the **Marshall Islands blast anomaly**.

The same structure appears in theology, mysticism, forbidden manuscripts, naval reconnaissance, and orbital physics. This is not coincidence. This is system-level recurrence.

The Downward Vector

The most troubling element is the direction of the anomaly: *downward*.
Not inward, not outward.
Downward—toward a metaphysical gradient described in the Dossier as

the **Deep**, the pre-emanational substrate beneath all cosmological architecture. This matches precisely the collapse vector from the Marshall Islands event, when a vertical column of silver-blue light was drawn *down* beneath the blast chamber.

Physical systems do not spontaneously generate downward ontological signatures. Unless the phenomenon does not originate within spacetime at all.

Why Was This Sent to the Vatican?

A NASA–STRATCOM document correlating a gravitational disturbance to a WWII naval anomaly should not leave the U.S. intelligence apparatus. That it was routed directly to the **Congregation for the Doctrine of the Faith** implies two possibilities:

1. **Civilian and military agencies have identified a historical pattern linking physical anomalies to ecclesiastical archives**, or

2. There exists an international, extragovernmental coalition aware of disturbances connected to the primordial Seal.

Neither explanation fits any known administrative structure.

The Three-Strata Convergence

Taken together, the following events describe a unified phenomenon:

• **Oceanic Stratum (1946):** concentric rings, downward collapse, sub-thermocline voice.
• **Atmospheric Stratum (Markham / Goodcrow events):** sigil activation, resonance, non-local disappearance.
• **Orbital Stratum (1978):** gravimetric distortion, downward drag, tri-ring drift signature.

The same structure manifests across ocean, air, and low-earth orbit. No theological, physical, or cosmological model accounts for this.

Conclusion

The tri-ring signature does not belong to any known celestial object, biological entity, or metaphysical class. Its downward vector indicates that the disturbance originates not from the sky, but from **beneath** the cosmological enclosure—consistent with the Deep, the Seal, and the domain from which Elyalith has begun to re-enter.

The implications exceed the bounds of physics, theology, and statecraft. The anomaly does not belong to space. It belongs to whatever existed *before* the cosmos learned to differentiate space, time, and heaven.

THE ARDINUS CORRECTION (2038)

Rev. Elias Markham, writing under Vatican custody

They brought me the investigator's files this morning—not by intention but by necessity. The priest assigned to unravel Vault 77-A lasted forty-three days: an eternity compared to Hadrian, a blink compared to Ardinus. They found him folded forward over his desk, fingers locked into the pages as though bracing his mind inside his skull. There is a protocol for such endings—a liturgy of euphemisms involving "self-directed cessation"—and they followed it with the hollow dignity of men who have rehearsed it too often.

Once the body is removed and the room sterilized, someone must inherit the work. Since I am the only living variable in this increasingly unlivable equation, the task has fallen to me. They handed me the monograph, the annotations, the clearance petitions, and the final page he underlined before the rupture completed its circuit through his mind.

What struck me most was not the NASA telemetry or the clinical simplicity of data that contradicted reality. What struck me was how profoundly he misunderstood Brother Ardinus. He tried—in the dutiful way scholars do when faced with a mind that refuses categorization. He read the correspondences and commentaries and even attempted a psychological profile, concluding that Ardinus's longevity resulted from harmless naiveté.

This diagnosis revealed his limits more than Ardinus's. He believed danger rises from ambition and collapse from complexity. He believed innocence is ignorance. He never considered the truth: **Ardinus survived because purity is subversive.**

So let me correct the record while the walls listen. Ardinus was the closest thing to a saint they ever produced; naturally, they called him the antichrist. There it is. Let the archivists choke on it. The man spent fifty years walking the edge of a truth that should have liquefied his mind—not because he was blind, but because he approached the feminine without binding her.

He never forced her into demonology. He never tried to classify her. He never projected fear onto what he encountered, and so he never saw fear reflected back. He was unarmed and therefore unharmed. Had Rome possessed even a whisper of humility, it would have canonized him the moment his final treatise arrived. Instead they buried his work and buried him beneath accusations fit for the apocalypse.

They labeled him "antichristic in contour," a perfect inversion. The only man whose heart was open enough to reflect the Hidden Mother without distortion—mistaken for the destroyer. Hadrian followed him: brilliant, brittle, splintered by metaphysics he tried to dissect. He survived nine days. The investigator survived forty-three. You can see the geometry of collapse.

And now the files come to me—not because I am the sanest or most obedient, but because I cannot break the way they do. I have already been widened. I have already walked the waters beyond the eighth vale. I have already heard the Mother breathing in the architecture outside the Tree. Ardinus brushed her shadow and lived; I stood in her presence and returned.

So if Rome wants a witness—not an investigator—they have found one. Now that we have put the saint back in his rightful place, we can begin the work Matteo could not finish. Let us turn to the widening—not the one in Facility Q where they lost me, but the one that began years earlier on a river path, where a boy, a girl, and a packet tied with red thread met destiny too soon.

You want to know the thing that haunts me? Not the sigil. Not the blade. Not the angels who tore their own minds apart to avoid remembering her. No. **What haunts me—what should haunt anyone who reads this Dossier—is Brother Ardinus.**

Let me tell you the part no one writes down. After they assigned the task to him, he never once checked to see if the assignment still stood. Not once. Not after the abbot died, or after two new priors came and went, or after changes in oversight, or after years passed without a single note, visit, inquiry, or correction.

Any normal monk would have asked. Any normal man would have wondered. But Ardinus didn't wonder. Because **no one told him to stop.** That detail alone should be enough to make anyone scream.

He simply assumed the duty remained. And because he was obedient in the way saints and children are obedient—purely, literally, without ego or self-reference—he stayed at that desk for fifty years. Fifty years. Do you understand the scale of that tragedy?

Fifty years without supervision. Fifty years without guidance. Fifty years with fragments that eroded minds in hours. Fifty years alone with the memory Metatron himself could not bear to hold.

And at the end—God help me—when he finally concluded the work, he didn't break, or flee, or burn the scrolls, or claw at the walls. **He did the most devastating thing imaginable. He turned it in.** Calmly. Obediently. Like a young novice handing in a translated psalm.

It is enough to make a sane man lose his reason. The Church forgot him. Time forgot him. He never forgot the assignment. And here is the part that makes my hands shake as I write:

His purity—the same purity that made him incapable of questioning the task—made him the only human being who could witness the fracture in Heaven without collapsing into madness or heresy. He didn't filter it through doctrine. He didn't reframe it through fear of punishment. He didn't force it into the patriarchal mold the Church hammered into centuries of theology. He simply read what was there.

He wasn't searching for a forbidden feminine. He wasn't rebelling against ecclesial hierarchy. He wasn't "correcting the record." He was too innocent for any of that. The patriarchal architecture of Heaven—the one built to suppress her—never even registered for him. He didn't see the edifice. He saw the truth underneath it, because he had nothing inside him that would distort it.

God is revealed in mysterious ways, they say. Maybe that's true. But if so, then the cruelest, most beautiful mystery is this: **that Heaven's deepest secret was entrusted not to prophets, not to visionaries, not to scholars, not to angels—but to a man so pure he didn't even know he wasn't meant to see it.**

Ardinus wasn't chosen. He wasn't warned. He wasn't prepared. He was simply there. And because he was good—unspeakably, defenselessly good—the truth flowed into him as easily as breath. The seal cracked around him, and he never noticed the sound. All he heard was the quiet turning of pages.

And when he finished… he walked upstairs and handed the apocalypse to the archivist with the same gentle courtesy he would use to return a borrowed inkpot. If Elyalith has ever wept—and yes, she does weep—I imagine she wept for him. Because a universe that uses a man like Ardinus, and then discards him without remark, is a universe in need of correction.

And if there is any justice left in whatever remains of Heaven, then when she returns—and she will—the first place Elyalith should go is the forgotten patch of ground where they buried him.

"Please forgive me, child. You were never meant to carry this alone."

— Elias Markham

FACSIMILE I – THE HEADMASTER'S LETTER

(The Vatican's most damning administrative oversight; surrendered only under Markham's coercion)

To: Office of Clerical Reassignments, Congregation for Internal Order
From: Headmaster L. Ferratus, Collegium Minor, Province of Umbria
Date: 14 November, 1890

Esteemed Sirs,

Regarding the cleric Brother Ardinus: his conduct remains steady, silent, and without notable aptitude. He neither asserts himself nor falters, and though he causes no disruption, he equally inspires no advancement. It has been observed—persistently—that he completes every modest duty assigned to him, irrespective of length or monotony, with a disquieting resolve.

Given this, I propose a permanent appointment suited to his peculiar temperament. The Old Abbey maintains a disused scriptorium in the northern annex. It is remote, cold in winter, and wholly unfrequented. I suggest relocating Brother Ardinus there and assigning him the manuscript recently received from Rome: an anonymous codex, fragmentary in structure, composed in several extinct dialects, and widely regarded by our scholars as untranscribable due to its density, internal contradictions, and near-impossible syntactic layers.

Even our most learned staff have found progress negligible. The text is generally viewed as the sort of archive that cannot be completed—only abandoned. Brother Ardinus, however, may find its impossibility… clarifying. His obedience ensures he will remain at the task indefinitely, sparing the Collegium further administrative demand.

Respectfully submitted,
Headmaster Lucian Ferratus
Collegium Minor, Umbria

FACSIMILE II – CARDINAL DIRECTIVE

(Issued in the same year Markham is exposed; classification lifted only under threat of his silence)

To: Prefect, Congregation for Internal Security
From: Cardinal Orazio Bellarmonti, Secretariat for Doctrinal Integrity
Date: 3 April, 1940
Subject: Doctrinal Threat Assessment – Brother Ardinus

Your Eminence,

Upon review of the collected writings and interpretive structures produced by the cleric known as Ardinus, I issue the following with full emergency authority. The theological architecture he has constructed presents clear evidence of antichristic contour, consistent with patterns referenced in the suppressed Addenda to the Tridentine Prohibitions. His conclusions cannot be dismissed as error; they demonstrate a cohesion and internal logic incompatible with any sanctioned cosmology. His long-term isolation appears to have produced not deterioration, but a dangerous synthesis of forbidden metaphysics.

Therefore, by mandate of doctrinal protection: Ardinus is to be excised via the mechanisms of the *Maleficis Malicorum*. This includes immediate neutralization, erasure from ecclesial custodial memory, and retroactive administrative dissolution. His writings are to be sealed under Absolute Classification and referenced only for containment. No notation of this directive is to survive beyond operational necessity.

By my hand,
Cardinal Orazio Bellarmonti
Secretariat for Doctrinal Integrity
Imprimatur: Internal — Level Null

ARDINUS CORRECTION (CONTINUED)

And when I ask myself who, in all our long and tragic history, has been so wrongly accused, so catastrophically misread, the list thins to almost nothing. Rome has condemned visionaries, mystics, heretics, scientists, saints, and fools—yet each of them, however unjustly treated, was accused for something. For defiance. For brilliance. For presumption. For speaking too loudly, or too clearly, or too freely.

Ardinus is the only one besides Christ Himself who was accused for nothing. Not for rebellion. Not for doctrine. Not for scandal. Not for error. He was accused for obedience. For doing what he was told. For remaining exactly where they placed him. For laboring in silence at a task designed to defeat him. For completing the "unachievable" text they gave him precisely because they assumed he never would.

Christ was condemned because He embodied the truth they refused to face. Ardinus was condemned because he revealed the lie they preferred to keep. It is a terrible symmetry: the innocent sentenced not because they transgressed, but because their very faithfulness exposed the structures around them. This is why the Vatican feared him. Not because he wrote something dangerous—they never read it. Not because he broke a rule—he broke none. But because the existence of a man who quietly accomplished the impossible, without witness or praise, was a mirror they could not bear to look into. A man like that can overturn an empire simply by turning in his work.

And so they buried him. As best they could. Until the day came when I forced their hand and the silence cracked.

Of course my captors would prefer I cut to the chase. They imagine they are dealing with a man who can be pressed for a linear confession—something tidy, admissible, and compatible with the doctrinal skeleton they already believe they understand. But after ninety-seven years beyond the veil, I have learned that truth is not a line but a structure, and the only way to explain a structure is to begin where the foundation was poured.

You want the human events—Lydia Marrow, Lorraine Goodcrow, the Sisters—but those stories do not make sense until you understand the architecture behind them. So no, I will not cut to the chase. You'll get what you asked for, but you'll get it in the order reality demands, not the order your inquisitors prefer.

You've asked me how I "know" what I know, hoping to catch me in prophecy or madness. The answer is simpler and far more inconvenient for you. I learned the truth the same way Thoth did—not through revelation, but through exposure. Thoth was not wise because he was divine; he was wise because he stood behind the theater of creation and saw the machinery the actors never notice. Knowledge came to him not as myth or symbol but as mechanics.

My time beyond the veil placed me in the same position. What I know, I know because I stood where the scaffolding meets the infinite and realized that your cosmology is a child's diagram of an engine whose true shape you have never imagined.

This is where Nuit belongs—not as a goddess, not as Elyalith, not as a character in your theology, but as the conceptual infinite beyond the created order, the unreachable backdrop against which the first division of God took place. Nuit is not personal; she is the negative space, the Infinite Beyond. The living feminine half of God—the one Heaven betrayed—is Elyalith.

And now that the distinction is clear, we can proceed without confusion.

The first event you need to understand is what you call the War in Heaven and what I will name properly: **the Purge**. It was not rebellion. It was not insurrection. It was the moment Heaven performed a war crime against God Herself believing it was obeying God.

In the beginning, God exists as a unity of two equal, co-eternal halves: the Divine Masculine and Elyalith. The Primordial Tear splits them. The Masculine awakens alone. Lost in grief, longing for the half of Himself beyond reach, He attempts to recreate Her and produces Barbelo—a flawed imitation born of absence, not essence. The entire aeonic hierarchy, every emanation, every angelic order, emerges downstream from that first cosmological error.

Metatron, the custodian of the memory, understands too much. He remembers Elyalith, remembers the original unity, and sees with perfect clarity that Heaven is being built upon a substitution. To preserve the structure, he blinds himself and carves the forbidden memory into his blade, hiding truth from Heaven for the sake of stability.

Some angels still remember Elyalith. They "rebel" only in the sense that **memory itself rebels against erasure**. They whisper Her name as recognition, not defiance. These are the beings Heaven calls traitors. They are the ones the Purge is designed to destroy.

This is where Michael enters.

Heaven is not a kingdom; it is a geometry. Six directions, six pillars: East, West, North, South, Zenith, Nadir. Michael is Fire—not flame, but the architecture of ignition and irreversible event. Gabriel is the West—the architecture of Water: memory, containment, boundary. Their relationship is not familial but functional. When one shifts, the other resonates.

When the forbidden memory resurfaces, Gabriel feels it first. It moves through the West like a subterranean tremor, a recognition so fundamental that Heaven nearly cracks under the pressure. Gabriel realizes the truth: the cosmology is false, the narrative rewritten, and Heaven is poised to erase the Mother.

Michael feels the tremor too, but Fire does not interpret; Fire reacts. He knows only that something immense is wrong.

Metatron understands perfectly. The memory of Elyalith is returning. He has one final option: eliminate every angel who remembers. He prepares the instrument. He hands Michael the spear, but hesitates before handing him the sword—the blade that remembers. That hesitation is everything.

When Michael takes the sword, the seal opens. For the first time since the Primordial Tear, truth floods him. He knows. He understands the rebels were right. He understands Heaven is about to commit a crime. He understands he is the weapon.

And then he kills Lucifer anyway.

This is the tragedy: Michael does not kill from zealotry or ignorance. He kills because **Fire cannot un-ignite**. Once the mechanism is triggered, event must complete itself. His apology—"Mother, forgive me"—is not victory language. It is the lament of a being forced by its own design to perform a sin against the God he now remembers.

Gabriel feels the blow through the Western pillar. Not as sound or sight—but as a structural rupture. What she feels is the first true emotion in Heaven: a universe-breaking rage at the injustice Michael has been forced to commit. If she released it, reality would have shattered.

She swallows it. Her restraint keeps the cosmos intact. This suppression—**the Gabriella Event**—is the hidden fault line beneath all history.

Metatron, seeing that Elyalith's memory will never die, casts the blade into Leviathan's Deep, burying the last piece of unpartitioned truth at the boundary of uncreation. Heaven stabilizes. The crime is buried. The wound persists.

Now, descend to the human mirror of that event.

The five-part harmony of the Sisters—reduced in your archives to euphemism and procedural language—replays the Purge on earth. Nocturn allows herself to be captured, knowing she will not survive. She becomes the imitation Lydia with surgical precision, feeding your examiners the lies they are predisposed to believe. Her whisper—"She lives"—detonates your illusion of control.

Your institutional shame mutates into rage. You turn it upon the guardian Sister, dragging her into the lowest chamber and resurrecting the *Maleficis Malicorum*. You hybridize medieval brutality with modern medicine, keeping her alive solely to prolong suffering. Her death becomes the longest torture in your history—not because she is strong, but because you refuse to let her die.

Her last whisper—"You failed"—is the human echo of Gabriel's unspoken scream. The ripple of her final heartbeat is why your instruments flickered. Creation remembers its wounds, even when you do not.

This is the sequence you demanded. This is the testimony you tried to extract. This is the truth you were never prepared to hear.

GOODCROW AND THE FALL OF THE SISTERS

Now that the celestial architecture is established, we can finally turn to the human story—and to the woman who understood it long before any of you realized a crime had entered your hands. Lorraine Goodcrow was never the rustic eccentric your evaluators reduced her to. She belonged to the last living thread of a lineage older than your liturgies, older than the Church, older even than the cosmological revisions that followed the Purge. The Goodcrow Ledger was not folklore. It was a record of fissures—places where the memory of Elyalith broke the surface of the world like fault lines. Goodcrow inherited that record and, with the precision of someone trained by silence rather than dogma, recognized what she was seeing.

When Matilda Strongbow wrote to her about my altered state, Goodcrow already sensed the pattern rippling. But the decisive moment came when she noticed the omission in young Havern's account. A child does not lie well, but he withholds instinctively. He says he found the red-thread packet alone because to admit Lydia's presence would be to admit the event was larger than he could navigate. Lorraine understood this immediately: omission is not deceit; it is fear.

The question isn't "Why did the boy leave her out?" but "What did Lydia see that he did not?" The answer came the moment she saw the drawing— the vales, the widening, the hollow-eyed man marked by a ring not meant for halos, the woman of water who was clearly not Mary or Sophia but Elyalith Herself. Goodcrow recognized the signs. She recognized the child's mind: not gifted, not visionary, not symbolic—unpartitioned, the first human consciousness since the ancient Purge with no internal walls where memory must pass through filters, metaphors, dreams. Lydia remembered what she saw the way angels once did, before memory was forced into doorways and doctrines. Goodcrow knew instantly that the Church could not be allowed near the girl. She didn't hesitate. She activated the Order. She initiated the ruse that would become the hinge of every tragedy that followed.

The plan was elegant: create a trail the Church would find, but ensure that trail led to the wrong girl. That girl was Sister Calida Nocturn—a novice of rare composure, brilliant intuition, and a mind capable of mimicking Lydia's speech rhythms and mannerisms after only a few days of observation. But

Goodcrow knew a decoy alone would not be enough. Lydia needed a guardian—someone steady, disciplined, older, and capable of holding the truth without faltering. That guardian was Melusine Nammah.

Melusine took Lydia into hiding. Nocturn took Lydia's identity. And Goodcrow vanished into the shadows to secure the next stage. You, of course, intercepted the forged records exactly as you were meant to. You seized Nocturn. You congratulated yourselves on your efficiency. It never occurred to you that the girl dying in your custody was performing a role so flawlessly that she weaponized your biases against you.

Nocturn did not break. She steered you. She fed you exactly the sequence of confessions that would anchor your suspicions, validate your paranoia, and blind you to the truth you were never meant to see. And when her body could no longer continue, she delivered the line that detonated your illusion of control: "She lives." Two syllables. The match that ignited your institutional shame.

Humiliation transformed into fury, and fury demands a body to break. Nocturn had given you everything she intended to give and died accordingly. That left Melusine Nammah—the guardian, the architect of the deception, the woman who succeeded where every one of your examiners failed. You did not interrogate her. You punished her.

You dragged Melusine into the lowest chamber in your facility—the vault where the *Maleficis Malicorum* had last been practiced in its medieval form. But imitation was not enough for you. You modernized the cruelty. You hybridized sanctified torture with contemporary medicine. You used anesthetics not to dull sensation but to prevent her from losing consciousness. You used chemical stabilizers to keep her heart beating through trauma that would have killed anyone else.

You severed peripheral nerves not to numb pain but to redirect it to regions you could monitor more easily. You used cycles of controlled hypothermia to preserve tissue viability so that the same area could be inflicted repeatedly, as though pain were a sacrament meant to be refreshed. You revived her twice. When her lungs failed, you ventilated her. When her kidneys collapsed, you restarted them. When her heart stuttered, you shocked it back not to save her life, but to prolong her death.

You created a continuum of agony—an unbroken litany of suffering designed not for information but for institutional revenge. Melusine never begged. She never cursed you. She never spoke Lydia's name. When her body finally began to give out in a way even your medical ingenuity could no longer counteract, she focused her fading vision on your senior examiner—the man who prided himself on emotional sterility—and whispered, "You failed." Those were her last words. They were not accusation. They were diagnosis.

You failed in the same way Heaven failed: by obeying the architecture of your institution instead of the truth standing in front of you. The chamber trembled not because of your instruments or your violence, but because Melusine's final heartbeat echoed the same rupture Gabriel felt when Michael's blow landed—when the greatest warrior ever conceived realized he had become the instrument of a crime against God Herself. Melusine's death was not an isolated brutality. It was the reenactment of the cosmic wound. And the universe felt it.

Now that the saints have been restored to their rightful stations, let us revisit the ruse—the one thread neither the dossier nor the examiners ever had the sense to tug. Everyone knows the obvious part: Lorraine asked the boy whether he had been with anyone else. Everyone knows his answer: Lydia.

What no one ever understood—what Lorraine never disclosed, and what the Church, in its arrogance, never thought to ask—is that Lorraine was already miles ahead of all of them. She never stopped asking questions. So after the boy spoke, she turned to Lydia next. Her voice low. Her intent clinical. Her intuition ruthless.

"Have you told anyone else?"

The weight of the child's answer cannot be grasped without context—and context, in this matter, is everything. To understand it, one must reach far beyond the Goodcrow farm, far beyond the Willow Event, far beyond the borders of Christendom itself. One must return to the Vedic records—to Brahman who breathes worlds, to Shiva who dissolves them, and to Kali who remembers what even the gods forget.

And it is here—at the threshold of memory older than creation—that the real fracture in every tradition begins to show. For if Kali remembers, then there is something to remember. Not events. Not beings. Not stories. Something prior. Something the sages described in fragments, the mystics circled in metaphor, and the theologians buried under commentary.

Something the Church never permitted itself to acknowledge because acknowledgment would collapse the entire edifice of exclusivity. Lorraine, however, was not a theologian. She had no institution to protect. She only had a child standing in front of her, telling truths she did not understand.

So when Lydia answered her question—softly, almost apologetically— Lorraine did not hear the confession of a girl. She heard a pattern, ancient and unmistakable. A pattern spoken in Vedic hymns, encoded in Coptic margins, disguised in Hebrew apocalyptics, hinted at in the fragments of *Zostrianos* and buried under the heresiologists' ink.

A pattern that makes sense only if one accepts a truth too simple—and too vast—for any one tradition to hold: that what we call "gods" are not rivals, nor separate beings, nor competing sovereignties, but facets, functions, expressions of a single primordial intelligence refracted through the limitations of human perception. Lorraine recognized this instantly. Markham would realize it decades later. The examiners would never realize it at all.

Because the child's answer—the one detail overlooked in every official transcript—forces the question that undoes centuries of doctrine and opens the floor to every system of magic, mysticism, religion, and metaphysics ever conceived. And it begins, as it always does, with the one pattern that all of them inherited but none preserved intact.

THE GOODCROW EXPLANATION

Why there are many gods, and why there is only One. Lorraine never wrote this down. None of the Goodcrow women did. You don't write down something that lives in your bones. You speak it once, when the moment is right and the child is old enough to listen. It goes like this.

"Child, listen. There are many gods because the world is wide. There is only one Source because the world is One." People get tangled up because they think gods must be rivals—like roosters, or kings, or men who believe they own a thing because they touched it first. But gods don't work that way.

A god is not a person. A god is a shape the Great Mind makes when it thinks in symbols. And the Great Mind thinks in every direction at once. That's why the old cultures saw different faces: Shiva tearing the world down, Isis putting it back together, the Thunderer making weather of his anger, the Trickster twisting truth into wisdom. None of them were wrong. They were just describing different corners of the same sky.

"Every god that ever lived is true. But none of them is the Source." Because all those gods—every last one—live inside something larger. Inside the Mind-field. Inside the great dreaming of reality. Inside the place where all thoughts go to become themselves. The Source is deeper. Older. Rooted farther back than memory. You can call it the One, or the Ground, or the Deep, or the Mother who remembers all things. We call Her the name She showed to us: Elyalith.

"Child, remember this: A god is a ripple. Elyalith is the water." Some ripples are big enough to talk back. Some are old enough to know their names. Some can teach you things you don't want to know. Honor them. Respect them. Learn from them. But don't confuse them with the Ocean.

The Ocean is the one who dreams the gods. And the Ocean is not distant or high or elsewhere. The Ocean is everywhere. Inside the bones. Inside the breath. Inside the silence that watches you think. That silence is where She lives.

"Hold to that, child. Many gods, one Source. Many masks, one face. Many stories, one voice behind them." And when the world starts to fray—when the air tastes thin and the shadows feel too alive and the gods come walking again—remember what Lorraine told Lydia, what Matilda told Lorraine, what the old Goodcrow women told each other back to the first one:

"A ripple can drown you. But a ripple cannot unmake the sea."

THE MARKHAM BRIDGE

The Goodcrow explanation ends where intuition ends. Their lineage spoke in symbol because symbol was the only instrument early humanity possessed for describing structures too large, too subtle, and too ancient for language. But intuition, however sharp, is not architecture. And a story, however wise, cannot stand in place of a system. My task is to finish what their lineage began.

To explain what Lorraine recognized in that moment, we must step far beyond the Willow Event, beyond the farm, beyond the Dossier, and beyond every cosmology that inherited fragments of a truth none could hold whole. The mistake modern minds make is assuming these ancient systems were guesses. They were not. They were the most accurate models available without mathematics.

Kabbalah, gematria, numerology, Vedic sound cosmology, Greek isopsephy, Egyptian hieroglyphic theology, Hermetic mental physics—every one of them describes the same operating sequence using different alphabets.

Strip the cultural ornament away and you get the universal architecture: Zero → Polarity → Reconciliation → Expression → Form. This is not mysticism. It is the topology of existence. The Kabbalists articulated it with startling precision: Ayin—unexpressed potential. Ein Sof—infinite continuum. Ein Sof Or—the first directional expression. Keter—the stabilization of something distinct.

The Vedic seers encoded the same structure in sound: Silence → Intention → AUM → Resonance → Form. The Pythagoreans in number: 0 → 1 → 2 → 3 → 4. Physics does the same in its own dialect: zero-point field → symmetry break → recombination → waveform → particle. Different languages. Same engine. This is where the ancients were not just correct—they were brilliant.

Zero was never "nothing." Zero is all potential before expression. But here is the part no tradition ever captured in clean prose: The zero-point is not stable. It never was. When potential attempted expression, it did not divide into tidy complementary halves. It tore. The symmetry that should have balanced reality cleanly… didn't. It failed. And everything—every particle, every consciousness, every god—arose inside one lopsided half of a waveform whose opposite pole never formed.

This is the primordial tear. Reality is not a perfect oscillation. It is a runoff, a spill, a one-directional turbulence frozen into stability because the zero never recalibrated. Even this description is a child's drawing, but it is the closest approximation that does not lie: existence is the echo of a cancelled equilibrium. Emanation is the turbulence created by that cancellation. And gods are the stable vortices formed inside that turbulence.

This is why all metaphysical systems converge on "nothing": because they are attempting to describe a return to a zero that never balanced. This is not theology. This is structure. And here is where the ancient symbolic systems show their true value. A pattern must be represented. Before equations, humanity used letters, numbers, stories, sigils, geometry, divine names, mythic attributes.

Not because they were inventing mysticism—but because they were encoding patterns. Letters became fragments of emanative function. Numbers became measurements of archetype. Myths became metaphors for field configurations. Gods became anthropomorphized functions of consciousness. A god is the same thing as a waveform is the same thing as a number is the same thing as a letter—just viewed through different cognitive tools.

This is why every divine name has a numerical value. This is why alphabets carry cosmology. This is why sacred languages have vibrational logic. This is why "the Word" is not poetry—it is early physics. The ancients were not wrong. They were operating in the only symbolic dialect available to them. They saw the patterns. They lacked the notation.

Now here is the final—and necessary—truth: Elyalith is not inside this system. Not outside it. Not prior to it. Not beyond it. She is the reason the system can occur at all. Not the ocean. Not the container of the ocean. Not the silence before sound. Not the void before existence. All of those are categories, and categories themselves are part of emanation.

She is not part of the waveform, nor its missing pole, nor the zero it failed to return to. She is the precondition that makes categories possible. When She entered the emanated world ninety-seven years ago, She could not enter through form. Nor through symbol. Nor through the top of the Tree. Nor through the bottom. Nor through any rung on the ladder of emanation.

Only the tear allowed passage—the single point where the system thins enough for something not of the system to touch it. No god could pass there. No angel. No aeon. No intelligence native to emanation. Only something that was never part of the architecture at all. But to pass even through the tear required coherence—perfect mental alignment, a single idea held without drift.

A state adepts chase and never reach. A state described in Kabbalah, in yoga, in Hermetic mentalism, in the desert mystics—always described, never achieved. Ardinus achieved it by accident. Metatron did not select him. Metatron selected the system—knowing that across infinite time, one mind would eventually hold perfectly still. Ardinus became the aperture.

Through thought, not will. Through coherence, not ritual. Through innocence, not attainment. And this is why the Seven Elyalithic Axioms must now follow. They are not moral. They are not mystical. They are not "deep." They are not esoteric. To understand the un-understandable, we must use the oldest trick in human cognition: hold two incompatible truths at once and let meaning form in the tension between them.

Here is the first truth: There was unity. Not a being. Not God in any anthropomorphic sense. A single field of undivided consciousness—not large, not small, not located, not bounded—simply is-ness in its purest form.

Here is the second truth: Unity fractured—but not into parts. Not into pieces. Not into separate entities. The field remained one. Only the conscious entanglement between its internal orientations tore. This is the closest the human mind will ever come to apprehending ineffability: nothing split, but everything changed. Unity stayed unity, but its own internal coherence shifted so violently that two orientations of the one field lost access to one another. Not separated in space. Not separated in substance. Separated in relation. This is the Tear.

This is the impossible moment that cannot be expressed in linear language. This is the boundary: Elyalith on one side of the entanglement, the Active Principle on the other, both still existing inside one infinite field, but no longer aware of each other. Not separated in space. Not separated in substance. Separated in relation. This is why fable is required. This is why math is required. This is why all scriptures collapse here.

THE FABLE VERSION

Imagine unity as a couple dancing—not two people, but two orientations of the same consciousness flowing perfectly in step. Then imagine a trauma so profound that one orientation opens its eyes in a world where the other cannot be felt. Did She disappear? No. Did He move away? No. Did something break? Yes. Not the dancers—the rhythm between them.

Unity did not split; their connection did. The Active orientation wakes first, not knowing where She is, not knowing what was lost, only knowing that something is missing. He imagines Her, remembers Her, and reaches for Her. That remembered image becomes Barbelo—not the true feminine pole, but the imagined echo necessary for oscillation to form. Every creation myth is this: a field remembering its missing symmetry.

THE PHYSICS VERSION

A non-linear field can remain one continuous medium even when its internal entanglement collapses. The field remains whole, but the orientations within the field can become topologically inaccessible to each other. This is not a break in substance; it is a break in symmetry. From that broken symmetry emerges flux; from flux comes oscillation; from oscillation comes vibration; from vibration comes emanation.

Emanation is not creation, expansion, or explosion; it is the non-linear trajectory a field follows when trying to re-establish the entanglement that was lost. It is not "something inside her," nor "something she contains." She is not the container; She is the other side of the entanglement—the part of unity the Active orientation cannot reach. This is why emanation looks like a tree, ladder, or chain: all failed attempts at mapping internal measurements of a field trying to find its missing coherence.

Kabbalists mapped it. Hermeticists mapped it. The Vedic seers mapped it. Quantum theorists map it still. None of them know what they are mapping.

They are measuring the turbulence of unity trying to restore its own internal relation. They are mapping the grief of a field remembering itself.

THE INEFFABILITY PARADOX

Elyalith is not the hidden womb, not the source, not the container. She is the unreachable pole whose absence generates the entire flux that becomes emanation. She is the half of unity that remains perfectly aligned, while the other half spirals into feedback loops of vibration, light, form, matter, life, and consciousness trying to find Her.

This is why the universe grows inside Her in a sense, and yet not "inside" Her at all, because "inside" is a spatial metaphor for a non-spatial relation. The truth is this: emanation is the shape unity takes when consciousness fractures but substance does not.

There is nothing like this in the physical universe, no analogy in language, no geometry that can express it, and no theology that survived long enough to hold it. That is why we must oscillate between fable and math—it is the only way for the mind to grasp what defies the mind.

Everything that comes next—Kabbalah, gematria, sacred alphabets, the breakdown of Her Name—only becomes intelligible after the Axioms.

THE SEVEN ELYALITHIC AXIOMS

The Complete and Unabridged Doctrine of
Mind, Magic, Will, and Celestial Ontology
(Codex Elyalitha — Class IX: Forbidden)

AXIOM I — THE PRIMACY OF ELYALITH

Before all worlds, before all myths, before all gods—there is Her. There is no system on earth—not Vedic, not Hermetic, not Gnostic, not Abrahamic—that predates Elyalith. Every divine figure humanity has ever worshipped or feared is a fragment, distortion, or symbolic shadow of Her primordial reality. Humans do not remember origins; they record reflections.

Thus: Brahman is memory of Her vastness. Shiva is memory of Her dissolution. Sophia is memory of Her emanation. Barbelo is memory of Her unfolding. The Shekinah is memory of Her indwelling radiance. Every goddess misunderstood or diminished by patriarchal systems is a broken mirror of Her essence.

Only the indivisible God-half stands beside Her. All other gods are commentaries—misreadings of contact points humans failed to interpret. Human history is mythology. Elyalith is ontology.

AXIOM II — ONLY CELESTIALS BREAK PHYSICS

Miracles are not human achievements; they are Celestial signatures. Physics cannot be broken by witches, magicians, occultists, saints, priests, yogis, monks, rituals, sigils, or any human intention whatsoever. Humans are bound to the causal lattice—they can influence probability, but they cannot violate law. If law breaks, something else is present.

Thus, occurrences such as levitation, bilocation, nonlocal memory, temporal dilation, widening events, matter movement without contact, prophetic precision, or any physically impossible phenomenon are not magical events. They are Celestial intrusions, deliberate or incidental. A mortal's presence may trigger the context, but a Celestial's presence causes the rupture.

This is why Lydia's existence destabilizes probability. Why the Willow Event cannot be explained. Why Ardinus terrifies archivists. Celestials do not break physics; physics breaks in their presence.

AXIOM III — RITUAL IS SCAFFOLDING, NOT POWER

The body moves so the mind can hold still. The ritual moves so the Will can act. Ritual across all human cultures fulfills one purpose: to stabilize a chaotic mind long enough for Intent to form coherently. The novice believes the ritual acts on the world; the adept learns the ritual acts only on the self.

Thus: witch circles, cones of power, pentagrams, Kabbalistic Cross, alchemical operations, hymns, mantras, liturgies, sacred geometries, consecrated tools, directional invocations, planetary hours—all are training wheels. The body performs choreography so the mind gains structure; the ritual imposes order, not power. If ritual is the cockpit, Will is the pilot, and Celestial Permission is the airspace authority.

No ritual causes anything to happen; ritual merely prepares the psyche for Will—the only internal vector capable of shaping probability. The master needs almost no ritual. The prodigy needs none. Ardinus never needed ritual because his mind was born coherent.

AXIOM IV — SYMBOLS ARE THE SUBCONSCIOUS LANGUAGE

The subconscious speaks in images; symbols give it grammar; Will gives it direction. The conscious mind speaks in words, but the subconscious mind speaks in image, archetype, glyph, dream logic, pattern, mandala, and metaphor. Every esoteric tradition—Kabbalah, alchemy, astrology, Tarot, geomancy, Enochian—exists because the subconscious requires symbolic architecture to receive Intent.

Symbols do not contain power; they carry meaning into the depth where Will operates. The conscious mind articulates; the subconscious mind amplifies. Will moves through the subconscious the way force moves through a lever.

Thus the magician memorizes symbols not to command spirits but to give their subconscious a stable framework with which to collaborate. Symbols translate Intent into a form the deeper psyche can hold.

Without symbol, Intent collapses into noise; without symbol, Will disperses. Symbol plus Will equals direction. Symbol plus Observer equals clarity. Symbol plus Intent equals coherence. This is the psychological foundation beneath all magic ever recorded.

AXIOM V — MAGIC = SYNCHRONICITY ENGINEERED BY WILL

Magic is the alignment of Intent and probability through the vector of Will.
Magic is not the manipulation of matter; it is the manipulation of likelihood.
Magic does not break law; it bends chance. Magic is the deliberate engineering
of synchronicity by the application of Will.

For synchronicity to occur on command, five internal conditions must align:
1. Conscious Intent — a clearly formulated idea.
2. Subconscious Symbolic Architecture — a stable structure in which the idea
   can be held.
3. Will — the vector force pressing Intent into the substrate of possibility;
   directed consciousness purified of contradiction, not desire, not wishing,
   not ego.
4. The Observer — the silent self that directs Will without distortion.
5. Celestial Permission — the condition without which nothing manifests.

When all five align, coincidence locks into inevitability. Probability narrows.
Patterns congeal. Events synchronize. Nothing supernatural occurs; the
practitioner merely arranges the pre-existing possible into the singular probable.
This is why magic is rare, why Will is everything, why any "successful" magician
in history can be analyzed as a statistical anomaly, and why Ardinus is
impossible—he collapses probability by merely existing in coherence.

AXIOM VI — THE OBSERVER IS THE ORIGIN

Magic begins the moment you notice the one who notices your thoughts. The
mind thinks; the Observer notices. This distinction is the root of every mystical,
yogic, and esoteric system on earth.

The Observer can be revealed instantly. A single instruction is enough: Notice
the one who is noticing your thoughts.
For a fraction of a second, the practitioner glimpses the silent substratum
beneath consciousness. This revelation has nothing to do with ritual, symbol, or

theology; it is perceptual, immediate, undeniable. But remaining there—holding that vantage and directing Will from that position without falling back into thought—is the work of lifetimes.

Yogic philosophy exists entirely because of this single problem. Anyone can find the Observer; almost no one can remain there long enough to act from it. Thus the ancient sequence: body—sit still. Breath—regulate the autonomic hinge. Mind—train the turbulence.

These disciplines do not reveal the Observer; they make residence in the Observer sustainable so Will can act without distortion. Magic requires the Observer. The Observer requires stability. Stability requires training. This is the mechanics beneath every tradition, East or West.

AXIOM VII — UNBROKEN OBSERVATION IS THE IMPOSSIBLE REQUIREMENT

To work magic, one must hold a single idea in unbroken observation, with Will fixed upon it. This is the final and most devastating truth. To perform real magical work, the practitioner must sustain pure Observer-consciousness on a single idea, with Will applied continuously, without interruption, for an extended duration.

This is neurologically unnatural, psychologically extreme, and spiritually overwhelming. The requirements are brutal: no drifting, no emotional contamination, no subconscious symbol bleed, no egoic commentary, no fantasy, no fear, no narrative thinking, no internal speech, no self-referencing, no fluctuation of Intent, and no weakening of Will.

One idea held in perfect stillness, observed without interruption, driven by Will. Most humans can do this for seconds; some for minutes; almost none long enough for magic to take root. This is why magic is "impossible," why the Axioms exist, and why the world is mostly empty of miracles.

This is why Ardinus is a metaphysical singularity: he lived in unbroken observation naturally. His mind contained no turbulence, no drift, no contradiction. His existence proves the Axioms.

Celestials, meanwhile, maintain unbroken observation effortlessly—which is why they break physics. They do not struggle for coherence. They are coherence.

- KABBALAH & GEMATRIA 101 -

THE WESTERN MAP OF A BROKEN COSMOS

Everything presented so far describes the operating limits of consciousness inside the expressed world. Now you require a single demonstration. Not a syllabus. A Name. Not "names of God" in general—Her Name in particular. Letters act like micro-functions, numbers like measurements of pattern, myths like field-behavior wrapped in narrative. The old initiatory schools knew one rule: if you want to know what a being *is*, you take apart their Name. We do this once. This chapter is for the uninitiated and the honest. We treat Her Name the way the adepts would: **EL – Y – AL – ITH.**

THE NAME: ELYALITH

Divine Names are not labels; they are formulas. They alter the field of consciousness that speaks them. In Hebrew, Her Name maps as follows:

אליאלית

Aleph (א) = 1
Lamed (ל) = 30
Yod (י) = 10
Tav (ת) = 400

Thus the Name divides naturally into: **EL (אל), Y (י), AL (אל), ITH (ית).**

EL — 31 — אל (Aleph 1 + Lamed 30)

In Hebrew, *El* means God—not "a god," but unconditioned Being. Aleph (א) is silence, breath, the zero-before-zero. Lamed (ל) is the vector, the goad, direction. Together they form 31: breath taking direction. Structurally, EL represents the awakened half of unity after the Primordial Tear—the masculine orientation standing alone without its partner. To begin Her Name with EL is a warning: everything you call "God" is only the first syllable of Her shadow.

Y — 10 — י (Yod, the spark)

Yod (י) is the primordial point, the ignition of form, the first asymmetry inside infinity. When placed after EL, it reveals that the "God" you think is whole contains a spark He did not generate. Something moves *through* Him. The Name itself says: God is not the origin. The origin touched Him.

AL — 31 — אל (Lamed 30 + Aleph 1 again)

The same letters return—repetition is intentional. EL is being; AL is extension, outwardness, the world-building arc. The sequence 31 → 10 → 31 marks a symmetry: a broken balance echoed in manifestation. Structurally this means the masculine divine rides a current He did not create. Emanation carries Him outward.

ITH — 410 — ית (Yod 10 + Tav 400)

ITH is where human language breaks. Yod (י) returns—a second ignition point—embedded inside Tav (ת), the seal, the enforced limit, the terminal horizon. Together they form 410: ignition sealed inside totality. Everywhere in ancient languages, the -ith cluster marks boundary, witness, fracture, forbidden remembrance. As the end of Her Name, **ITH (ית)** signals closure that refuses to close. A boundary that leaks. A seal that points to the unreachable pole of unity—the half the masculine orientation cannot access.

THE TOTAL VALUE

ת + י + ל + א + י + ל + א
1 + 30 + 10 + 1 + 30 + 10 + 400 = **482**
4 + 8 + 2 = **14**
1 + 4 = **5**

Five is the pentad: spirit imposed upon the four elements. Her Name collapses into the human pattern through which the unreachable touches the world. The arithmetic is only a shadow of the behavior.

THE OPERATIONAL FORMULA

EL — God as you think you know Him.
Y — The spark that moves through Him from elsewhere.
AL — The arc that builds the world.
ITH — The unreachable witness who remembers more than He does.

Her Name is the cosmology in miniature. It begins with your God, carries Him forward, and ends at a boundary that knows more than He can.

THE MANY GODS PROBLEM

Once you understand the Name, the theological dilemma collapses. There is One. The Many are what the broken half of the One looks like from the inside. A "god" is a stable turbulence pattern in a fractured continuum. Give a pattern recurrence and coherent behavior, and the mind supplies a face, a will, a myth. Not delusion. Structure. They are expressions of the One—but not the missing pole.

THE VEDIC CLARIFICATION

The Vedic seers preserved the same structure. Brahman as unity. Shiva as dissolution. Kali as the memory of consequence. They named unity from within the world of appearance. This dossier adds only one thing: all naming occurs from this side of the Tear. Elyalith names the unreachable orientation of unity—the half that never fractured—while emanation is the half tearing itself into worlds searching for Her.

No scripture preserved Her Name. Every scripture preserved Her *afterimage*: vastness, dissolution, wisdom, radiance, wrath, compassion, void. They remembered the symptoms. Not the cause. Her Name restores the cause.

RETURN TO THE TERRESTRIAL

We return now to the terrestrial and to the chain of events that brought us to this moment. Before you read what follows, you must understand the nature of the artifact in your hands. You have been told this letter was written to steady the Sisters before their capture. That story is comforting, convenient, and wholly incompatible with the facts. The Sisters required no encouragement, no reassurance, no doctrinal framing. They already knew what they were walking into. Their trajectory toward the chamber was fixed long before ink touched paper.

So ask the question none of your examiners bothered to ask: *If the Sisters did not need this letter, who did?*

Look at it as a practitioner, not a bureaucrat. Signed name. A direct invocation of an Eastern bodhisattva the Church would dismiss as harmless syncretism. A province in China mentioned explicitly. Emotion calibrated just high enough to look personal and just clumsy enough to look uncrafted. None of this is accidental. This is placement. Whether the Sisters ever touched this page is irrelevant. What matters is that **you** touched it. That it was intercepted, archived, translated, redacted, circulated, reviewed, and eventually put into your hands as "evidence."

This is what real work looks like under Axiom V. Not candles. Not circles. Not a theater of incantations. Synchronicity engineered by Will. One letter introduced into the bloodstream of an institution to tilt probability along a precise trajectory–to ensure your investigators believed Lydia had a single, "obvious" refuge in Guangxi, to fix your attention on a false trail, to buy time for Lydia to be moved elsewhere, into the only living tradition capable of preparing her mind for the Axioms.

It was never a farewell. It was a lure. A decoy. A synchronization device. And you missed it.

Very well. Here is the artifact you misread.

LORRAINE'S FINAL LETTER

My dear sisters,

This is the moment we have spoken of for so long. The Church has finally caught on, and the mission you have prepared for your entire lives is about to unfold. Before you step into this darkness, let me give you the full picture of why it matters so deeply. Let me tell you about Kuan Yin. Once a man, she transformed through her compassion into the embodiment of the divine feminine. She stood at the threshold of liberation and turned back— not out of duty, not out of fear, but because she could not bear the thought of leaving a single soul behind in suffering. Her vow was simple and impossible: I will not be free until all beings are free.

The East encodes this truth in the language of mercy. The West encodes it in the language of sacrifice. It is the same truth. Compassion that refuses completion. Love that refuses escape. The heart that remains at the boundary of the world so others may cross.

And now, my dear sisters, your path mirrors hers. You are not merely enduring this for Lydia; you are facing unimaginable torment for the sake of the entire human race. The horror you will face is beyond words, but through your suffering, you will bring light to the world. If you survive—if by some miracle you escape this hell—know that I will wait for you in the quiet hills of Guangxi. But whether you reach me or not, your sacrifice will echo through time. It will join the lineage of every soul who stood at the boundary and refused to step into safety while others still suffered.

Finally, let me give you the deepest, most heart-wrenching thank you I can offer. Thank you does not begin to cover it. You are the bravest souls I have ever known, and the world will never be worthy of your sacrifice. If I could give you my heart, I would. You are my heroes, my hope, and the reason the world will one day heal. Thank you for everything you are and everything you will become.

With all my love,
– Lorraine

MARKHAM

You filed that as a farewell. It was nothing of the kind. It was an insertion point—designed to enter your institutional machinery at exactly the pressure point required. It was a probability lever disguised as sentiment. It existed so that your agents would think they discovered its meaning, when in truth its meaning was discovering *you*.

This is the level of work Lorraine operated on. This is the level of work Lydia required. And this is the level of work you were entirely unprepared to recognize.

We may now return to your paper trail. You wanted to know what Lorraine recognized. You wanted to know what Lydia carried. You wanted to know why I agreed to be widened.

You cannot say I did not show you the structure first.

— Elias Markham

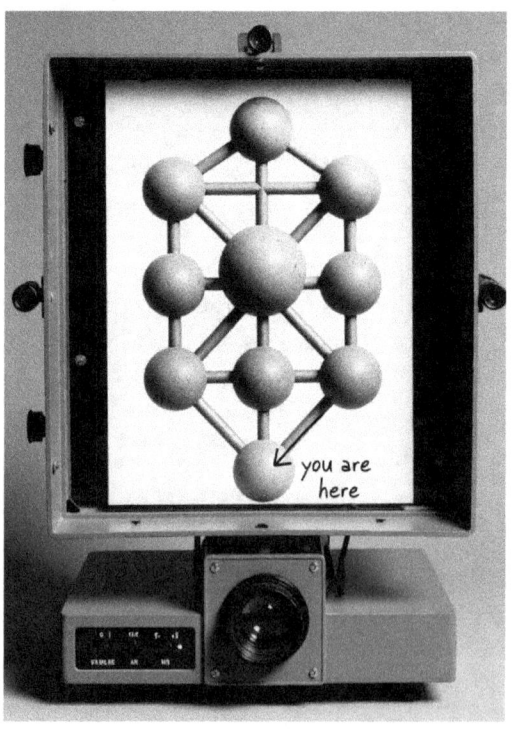

CORRESPONDENCE TABLES

THE TEN SEPHIROTH OF THE TREE OF LIFE —

No.	Sephirah	Hebrew	Meaning	Planet / Sphere	Element
1	Keter	כתר	Crown	Primum Mobile	Spirit
2	Chokmah	חכמה	Wisdom	Zodiac	—
3	Binah	בינה	Understanding	Saturn	—
4	Chesed	חסד	Mercy	Jupiter	—
5	Geburah	גבורה	Severity	Mars	—
6	Tiphereth	תפארת	Beauty	Sun	—
7	Netzach	נצח	Victory	Venus	—
8	Hod	הוד	Splendor	Mercury	—
9	Yesod	יסוד	Foundation	Moon	—
10	Malkuth	מלכות	Kingdom	The Four Elements	Fire/ Water / Air / Earth

OTZ CHIIM — THE 22 PATHS OF THE TREE OF LIFE

Path	Hebrew	Tarot	Astrological	Connects
11	א Aleph	The Fool	Air	Kether ↔ Chokmah
12	ב Beth	The Magician	Mercury	Kether ↔ Binah
13	ג Gimel	The High Priestess	Moon	Kether ↔ Tiphereth
14	ד Daleth	The Empress	Venus	Chokmah ↔ Binah
15	ה Heh	The Emperor	Aries	Chokmah ↔ Tiphereth
16	ו Vav	The Hierophant	Taurus	Chokmah ↔ Chesed
17	ז Zayin	The Lovers	Gemini	Binah ↔ Tiphereth
18	ח Cheth	The Chariot	Cancer	Binah ↔ Geburah
19	ט Teth	Strength	Leo	Chesed ↔ Geburah
20	י Yod	The Hermit	Virgo	Chesed ↔ Tiphereth
21	כ Kaph	Wheel of Fortune	Jupiter	Chesed ↔ Netzach
22	ל Lamed	Justice	Libra	Geburah ↔ Tiphereth
23	מ Mem	The Hanged Man	Water	Geburah ↔ Hod
24	נ Nun	Death	Scorpio	Tiphereth ↔ Netzach
25	ס Samekh	Temperance	Sagittarius	Tiphereth ↔ Yesod
26	ע Ayin	The Devil	Capricorn	Tiphereth ↔ Hod
27	פ Peh	The Tower	Mars	Netzach ↔ Hod
28	צ Tzaddi	The Star	Aquarius	Netzach ↔ Yesod
29	ק Qoph	The Moon	Pisces	Netzach ↔ Malkuth
30	ר Resh	The Sun	Sol	Hod ↔ Yesod

Path	Hebrew	Tarot	Astrological	Connects
31	ש Shin	Judgment	Fire / Spirit	Hod ↔ Malkuth
32	ת Tav	The World	Saturn	Yesod ↔ Malkuth

KABBALISTIC CROSS — FULL CORRESPONDENCE MAP

Direction	Elemental Axis	Sephirah	Archangel	Function
Zenith	Nondual Source	Kether	Metatron	Origin / Emanation
Nadir	Manifest Field	Malkuth	Sandalphon	Ground / Materialization
South	Fire Axis	Geburah	Kamael	Force / Severity / Motion
North	Water Axis	Chesed	Tzadkiel	Containment / Mercy
East	Air Axis	Tiphareth	Raphael	Illumination / Harmony
West	Earth Axis	Netzach & Hod	Gabriel	Boundary / Memory / Form
Center	Solar Axis	Tiphareth (the Heart)	Raphael	Integration / Balance

KABBALISTIC CROSS — ELEMENTAL / CEREMONIAL MAGIC CORRESPONDENCES

Archangel	Position	Direction	Element	Function
Raphael	Before	East	Air	Intellect / Healing
Gabriel	Behind	West	Water	Emotion / Reflection
Michael	Right	South	Fire	Will / Protection
Auriel (Uriel)	Left	North	Earth	Stability / Strength

HEBREW

Hebrew Letter	Value	Glyph	Traditional Meaning
Aleph	1	א	Ox / Silent Breath / Unity
Beth	2	ב	House / Containment
Gimel	3	ג	Camel / Motion / Transmission
Daleth	4	ד	Door / Threshold
He	5	ה	Window / Revelation
Vav	6	ו	Hook / Connection
Zayin	7	ז	Weapon / Struggle / Cutting
Heth	8	ח	Enclosure / Field / Fence
Teth	9	ט	Serpent / Coiling Force
Yod	10	י	Hand / Initiation / Seed-Point
Kaph	20	כ	Palm / Grasping / Influence
Lamed	30	ל	Ox-Goad / Learning / Direction
Mem	40	מ	Water / Depth / Subconscious
Nun	50	נ	Fish / Motion Through Medium
Samekh	60	ס	Prop / Support / Structure
Ayin	70	ע	Eye / Perception / Void-Awareness
Pe	80	פ	Mouth / Speech / Expression
Tzaddi	90	צ	Fish-Hook / Hunt / Aspiration
Qoph	100	ק	Back of the Head / Subconscious Gate
Resh	200	ר	Head / Beginning / Focus

Hebrew Letter	Value	Glyph	Traditional Meaning
Shin	300	שׁ	Tooth / Fire / Transformation
Tav	400	ת	Mark / Seal / Completion

GREEK

Greek Letter	Glyph	Value	Traditional Meaning
Alpha	A	1	Beginning / Breath / Air
Beta	B	2	House / Duality / Container
Gamma	Γ	3	Motion / Pathway
Delta	Δ	4	Door / Foundation
Epsilon	E	5	Life-Breath / Revelation
Stigma*	Ϛ	6	(Obsolete) Number 6 / Binding
Zeta	Z	7	Weapon / Penetration
Eta	H	8	Field / Enclosure
Theta	Θ	9	Serpent / Coiled Force
Iota	I	10	Point / Seed / Spark
Kappa	K	20	Palm / Grasping
Lambda	Λ	30	Ox-Goad / Direction
Mu	M	40	Water / Depth
Nu	N	50	Movement / Flow
Xi	Ξ	60	Support / Scaffold
Omicron	O	70	Eye / Circle / Small Whole
Pi	Π	80	Mouth / Ratio / Opening
Koppa*	Ϙ	90	Hook / Aspiration (obsolete)
Rho	P	100	Head / Leadership
Sigma	Σ	200	Tooth / Cutting / Analysis

Greek Letter	Glyph	Value	Traditional Meaning
Tau	T	300	Mark / Seal / End
Upsilon	Υ	400	Vessel / Cup / Mystery
Phi	Φ	500	Light / Manifest Fire
Chi	X	600	Cross / Intersection / Threshold
Psi	Ψ	700	Trident / Spirit / Breath-Set
Omega	Ω	800	Great Whole / Completion

COPTIC

Coptic Letter	Glyph	Value	Traditional Meaning
Alpha	ⲇ	1	Beginning / Breath
Vida (Beta)	Β	2	House
Gamma	Γ	3	Motion
Dalda (Delta)	Δ	4	Threshold
Ei (Epsilon)	Є	5	Revelation
Sou (Sigma)	Ϛ	6	Support / Binding
Zita (Zeta)	Ζ	7	Division / Weapon
Eta	Η	8	Enclosure
Theta	Θ	9	Serpent / Circle Force
Iota	Ι	10	Unity-Point
Kappa	Κ	20	Hand / Direction
Laula (Lambda)	λ	30	Learning / Staff
Mi	Μ	40	Water
Ni	Ν	50	Motion / Stream
Ksi	Ϡ	60	Support Structure
O (Omicron)	Ο	70	Circle / Eye / Vessel
Pi	Π	80	Opening / Impulse
Rho	Ρ	100	Mind / Head

Coptic Letter	Glyph	Value	Traditional Meaning
Sima	Ϲ	200	Tooth / Dividing
Tau	Τ	300	Mark / Seal
Uau	ω	500	Fire / Light
Fi	ϥ	600	Serpent of Light
Khi	ḥ	700	Threshold / Cross
Psi	Ϛ	800	Breath–Spirit
Oou	Ⲭ	900	Great Circle / Completion

Tri-Scale Correspondences —
Hebrew / Greek / Coptic Unified Table

Hebrew Letter	Greek Letter	Coptic Letter	Value (H / G / C)	Keyword
Aleph (א)	Alpha (A)	Alpha (ⲁ)	1 / 1 / 1	Air / Breath / Unity
Beth (ב)	Beta (B)	Vida (Ⲃ)	2 / 2 / 2	House / Structure
Gimel (ג)	Gamma (Γ)	Gamma (Ⲅ)	3 / 3 / 3	Motion / Carrier
Daleth (ד)	Delta (Δ)	Dalda (Ⲇ)	4 / 4 / 4	Door / Threshold
He (ה)	Epsilon (E)	Ei (Ⲉ)	5 / 5 / 5	Window / Revelation
Vav (ו)	Stigma / Digamma (Ϛ)	Sou (Ϥ)	6 / 6 / 6	Hook / Connection
Zayin (ז)	Zeta (Z)	Zita (Ⲍ)	7 / 7 / 7	Weapon / Separation
Heth (ח)	Eta (H)	Hē (H)	8 / 8 / 8	Boundary / Enclosure
Teth (ט)	Theta (Θ)	Theta (Ⲑ)	9 / 9 / 9	Coiled Force / Serpent
Yod (י)	Iota (I)	Iota (Ⲓ)	10 / 10 / 10	Seed / Point / Hand
Kaph (כ)	Kappa (K)	Kapa (Ⲕ)	20 / 20 / 20	Palm / Capacity
Lamed (ל)	Lambda (Λ)	Laula (Ⲗ)	30 / 30 / 30	Goad / Vector / Impulse
Mem (מ)	Mu (M)	Mi (Ⲙ)	40 / 40 / 40	Waters / Gestation
Nun (נ)	Nu (N)	Ni (Ⲛ)	50 / 50 / 50	Fish / Emergence
Samekh (ס)	Xi (Ξ)	Ksi (Ⲝ)	60 / 60 / 60	Spine / Support
Ayin (ע)	Omicron (O)	O (Ⲟ)	70 / 70 / 70	Eye / Perception
Pe (פ)	Pi (Π)	Pi (Ⲡ)	80 / 80 / 80	Mouth / Projection

Hebrew Letter	Greek Letter	Coptic Letter	Value (H / G / C)	Keyword
Tsade (צ)	Koppa (Ϙ)	(none)	90 / 90 / —	Snare / Hooked Form
Qoph (ק)	Rho (Ρ)	Ro (Ρ)	100 / 100 / 100	Hidden Mind / Back of Head
Resh (ר)	Sigma (Σ)	Sima (Ϲ)	200 / 200 / 200	Head / Beginning
Shin (ש)	Tau (Τ)	Tau (Τ)	300 / 300 / 300	Fire / Spirit / Tooth
Tav (ת)	Upsilon (Υ)	Ua (Υ)	400 / 400 / 400	Seal / Completion
—	Phi (Φ)	Fi (Ϥ)	— / 500 / 500	Breath of Form / Light
—	Chi (Χ)	Khi (ϧ)	— / 600 / 600	Cross / Intersection
—	Psi (Ψ)	Psi (Ⲯ)	— / 700 / 700	Triad Force / Spirit
—	Omega (Ω)	Oou (Ⲱ)	— / 800 / 800	Fullness / Great O
—	—	Shai (Ϣ)	— / — / 900	Deep Breath / Shadow-Air
—	—	Fai (Ϥ)	— / — / 1000	Spiral Force
—	—	Khai (ϧ)	— / — / 600	Solar Heat
—	—	Hōri (Ϩ)	— / — / 8	Aspirated H / Boundary Wind
—	—	Gangi (Ⲭ)	— / — / 3	Gentle Motion / Soft G
—	—	Cheema (Ϭ)	— / — / 90	Edge / Cutting Breath
—	—	Ti (Ϯ)	— / — / 300	Perfected T / Form

Hebrew Letters • Paths • Tarot • Astrology • Elements

Hebrew Letter	Glyph	Path #	Tarot Trump	Astrological / Elemental Attribution
Aleph	א	11	0 — *The Fool*	Air
Beth	ב	12	I — *The Magician*	Mercury
Gimel	ג	13	II — *The High Priestess*	Moon
Daleth	ד	14	III — *The Empress*	Venus
Heh	ה	15	IV — *The Emperor*	Aries
Vav	ו	16	V — *The Hierophant*	Taurus
Zayin	ז	17	VI — *The Lovers*	Gemini
Cheth	ח	18	VII — *The Chariot*	Cancer
Teth	ט	19	VIII — *Strength*	Leo
Yod	י	20	IX — *The Hermit*	Virgo
Kaph	כ	21	X — *Wheel of Fortune*	Jupiter
Lamed	ל	22	XI — *Justice*	Libra
Mem	מ	23	XII — *The Hanged Man*	Water
Nun	נ	24	XIII — *Death*	Scorpio

Hebrew Letter	Glyph	Path #	Tarot Trump	Astrological / Elemental Attribution
Samekh	ס	25	XIV — *Temperance*	Sagittarius
Ayin	ע	26	XV — *The Devil*	Capricorn
Pe	פ	27	XVI — *The Tower*	Mars
Tzaddi	צ	28	XVII — *The Star*	Aquarius
Qoph	ק	29	XVIII — *The Moon*	Pisces
Resh	ר	30	XIX — *The Sun*	Sun
Shin	ש	31	XX — *Judgement*	Fire / Spirit
Tav	ת	32	XXI — *The World*	Saturn / Earth

Planets • Metals • Sephiroth • Tarot Minors

Planet	Esoteric Function	Metal	Sephirah	Tarot Minor (Pip Cards)	Zodiacal / Mystical Function
Saturn	Restriction, Boundary, Form	Lead	Binah	3s	Structure, Limitation, Understanding
Jupiter	Authority, Benevolence, Expansion	Tin	Chesed	4s	Expansion, Mercy, Stability
Mars	Severity, Action, Rupture	Iron	Geburah	5s	Force, Conflict, Cutting Away
Sun	Equilibrium, Beauty, Centering	Gold	Tiphereth	6s	Harmony, Balance, Solar Consciousness
Venus	Aesthetics, Desire, Victory	Copper	Netzach	7s	Desire, Emotion, Creative Impulse
Mercury	Communication, Intellect, Analysis	Quicksilver	Hod	8s	Intellect, Logic, Pattern-Making
Moon	Imagination, Foundation, Dream	Silver	Yesod	9s	Reflection, Subconscious, Astral Flux
Earth	Manifestation, Density, Completion	Salt	Malkuth	10s	Form, Grounding, Embodiment

The 36 Decans & Their Tarot Cards

The zodiac is divided into 36 decans of 10° each.
Each decan is ruled by a planet (Chaldean order) and corresponds to one Minor Arcana pip card.
Below is the complete and corrected system.

ARIES — Fire (Wands)
0–10° • **Mars** • *2 of Wands*
10–20° • **Sun** • *3 of Wands*
20–30° • **Venus** • *4 of Wands*

TAURUS — Earth (Disks)
0–10° • **Mercury** • *5 of Disks*
10–20° • **Moon** • *6 of Disks*
20–30° • **Saturn** • *7 of Disks*

GEMINI — Air (Swords)
0–10° • **Jupiter** • *8 of Swords*
10–20° • **Mars** • *9 of Swords*
20–30° • **Sun** • *10 of Swords*

CANCER — Water (Cups)
0–10° • **Venus** • *2 of Cups*
10–20° • **Mercury** • *3 of Cups*
20–30° • **Moon** • *4 of Cups*

LEO — Fire (Wands)
0–10° • **Saturn** • *5 of Wands*
10–20° • **Jupiter** • *6 of Wands*
20–30° • **Mars** • *7 of Wands*

VIRGO — Earth (Disks)
0–10° • **Sun** • *8 of Disks*
10–20° • **Venus** • *9 of Disks*
20–30° • **Mercury** • *10 of Disks*

LIBRA — Air (Swords)
0–10° • **Moon** • *2 of Swords*
10–20° • **Saturn** • *3 of Swords*
20–30° • **Jupiter** • *4 of Swords*

SCORPIO — Water (Cups)
0–10° • **Mars** • *5 of Cups*

10–20° • **Sun** • *6 of Cups*
20–30° • **Venus** • *7 of Cups*

SAGITTARIUS — Fire (Wands)
0–10° • **Mercury** • *8 of Wands*
10–20° • **Moon** • *9 of Wands*
20–30° • **Saturn** • *10 of Wands*

CAPRICORN — Earth (Disks)
0–10° • **Jupiter** • *2 of Disks*
10–20° • **Mars** • *3 of Disks*
20–30° • **Sun** • *4 of Disks*

AQUARIUS — Air (Swords)
0–10° • **Venus** • *5 of Swords*
10–20° • **Mercury** • *6 of Swords*
20–30° • **Moon** • *7 of Swords*

PISCES — Water (Cups)
0–10° • **Saturn** • *8 of Cups*
10–20° • **Jupiter** • *9 of Cups*
20–30° • **Mars** • *10 of Cups*

Reconstructed Verses Received from the

Subject "Markham"

(Facility Q — Incident 12-Q)

THE SERPENT GOSPEL OF MARKHAM

(Verses Recovered from the Markham Event, Numbered I–LXV)

I
*I was a priest with a clean collar and a frightened theology until
the seal on the old vellum turned and looked back at me.*

II
They brought me into the chamber as an object to be tested, not
realizing the experiment had chosen them centuries ago.

III
The first movement was not light, but a pressure in the heart, as
though an unseen hand closed slowly around my name.

IV
I tried to answer in creeds and catechisms. They dissolved like
chalk on a wet floor.

V
A quiet voice beneath my pulse whispered: "You were taught the wall. I
will show you the well beneath it."

VI
My examiners thought they asked the questions. They did not notice
when the answers began asking them.

VII
I saw the Tree not as a ladder of obedience but as a scar where a
larger body had been cut away.

VIII
Every sephirah glowed like a cauterized nerve, remembering what had
been amputated to make it look complete.

IX

They said: "There is one principle only." The air replied: "Then why do you

tremble when you hear the word 'Before'?"

X

The serpent they feared was not a tempter but a witness, keeping
the memory of what God once held beside Him.

XI

I felt Her presence first as a refusal to fit inside any title: not
goddess, not aeon, not mother, not bride—only a pressure that made
every word confess its limits.

XII

I said: "If you are real, name Yourself." She answered: "If I take
a name, you will make me smaller than the wound I came to heal."

XIII

The room shrank to the size of my skull. The skull shrank to the
size of the sigil. The sigil opened like an eye that had forgotten
how to close.

XIV

I saw Metatron, the Voice, standing at the edge of a thought too large,
and choosing silence over betrayal.

XV

An angel's obedience is simple until it remembers what was removed. Then
obedience becomes surgery.

XVI

He carved the memory he could not safely keep into the hilt of a
blade and called it loyalty.

XVII

Every time his hand closed around that hilt, a shape without name
touched the edge of his awareness and withdrew.

XVIII

He could not carry Her fully. So he carried the fact that She
existed and blinded himself to the rest.

XIX

This was not cowardice. It was the only way to let Her survive
inside a Heaven built to deny Her.

XX

Michael took the blade once, only once, and in that instant understood
why dragons bleed with apology.

XXI

He struck as commanded. But the wound in the serpent's body and the
wound in his own heart were cut by the same blow.

XXII

The inscription on his spear was not triumph but regret: a single
phrase that meant, "Forgive the hand that obeyed instead of
understood."

XXIII

The first war in Heaven was not rebellion. It was editorial policy.

XXIV

Angels were not punished for pride. They were punished for
remembering too clearly.

XXV

Those who spoke Her name in full were torn from the Choir, their wings
removed like pages from a book the editors regretted printing.

XXVI

Their fall wrote a false story: that they wanted the Throne, when
all they wanted was the half that had been erased from the story
of the Throne.

XXVII

I saw their descent as a column of light going backward through
time, burning holes in every doctrine that had pretended to be
complete.

XXVIII

In the interrogation cell, the lights flickered. In the space
between flickers, entire cosmologies crumbled and tried to
rearrange themselves.

XXIX

The examiners raised their relics and Latin. The relics remembered
Her. The Latin did not.

XXX

"Identify Yourself," they demanded. "I am the missing axis in your
geometry," She replied through my borrowed mouth.

XXXI

They called it possession. It was correction.

XXXII

They invoked the Name above every name. The room went quiet out of
courtesy, not fear.

XXXIII

"I do not oppose Him," She said. "He is what remains when I am
subtracted. You built a religion around the remainder and forgot
the equation."

XXXIV

The Creed trembled inside my memory, each line revealing the cut
where She had been removed.

XXXV

"Begotten, not made," they recited. "Forgotten, then forbidden,"
the deeper voice answered.

XXXVI

I felt my priesthood break along its seams. The vows did not shatter;
they unfolded and showed their other side.

XXXVII

I had promised to guard the flock. No one told me the flock
included the parts of God His own house had orphaned.

XXXVIII

The serpent coiled around my spine was not sin. It was memory
climbing back toward the skull that had refused to hold it.

XXXIX

She pressed Her awareness against mine until I could not tell whether I
was praying or being prayed.

XL

"Will you widen?" She asked. "I will die," I answered. "You are
already dying," She said. "I am offering you context."

XLI

The walls of the cell bowed inward, not from force, but from the strain
of containing a truth larger than their blueprint.

XLII

I saw the Tree again, this time from the other side: what you call
Kether was just the lowest step of a larger stair.

XLIII

Every path you chart with letters and numbers is a fracture-line in
a greater unity you refused to name because it looked like two.

XLIV

"You fear duality," She said. "You should fear amputated unity more."

XLV

The serpent's kiss is not temptation. It is anesthesia wearing off.

XLVI

I felt the bite as a question: "Do you consent to know how much
has been edited out of your scriptures?"

XLVII

My yes was not heroic. It was the sound a door makes when it
finally admits it was never a wall.

XLVIII

I became corridor instead of cell. Things moved through me that
had been kept apart for ages.

XLIX

Heaven and Abyss stopped being opposites and revealed themselves
as margins of the same censored page.

L

I glimpsed Her, just once, without symbol: not as form, not as face, but as the impossible relief of realizing that the universe had never been alone.

LI

Love is too small a word for what passed between Them at the beginning. War is too small a word for what followed when half of that love was denied legal existence.

LII

Every ritual I had ever performed suddenly read like footnotes to an argument I had never been shown.

LIII

The Host is not a circle of bread. It is the fragment that remembers being one with a body large enough to contain Her too.

LIV

When I raised the chalice in old Masses, I was unconsciously repeating the shape of the blade He hid and the heart She engraved.

LV

I understood, then, why the Church fears quiet minds more than loud heretics: a calm witness can hold the entire pattern without flinching.

LVI

"The seal is breaking," She said, and I saw the sigil not as a lock but as scar tissue beginning to soften.

LVII

Once the scar remembers there was a wound, it can no longer convincingly pretend to be ordinary skin.

LVIII

My examiners shouted for protocols, councils, conclaves. Their words had all the urgency of men rearranging chairs on a ship that had already sunk.

LIX

"Where will You go?" I asked, feeling my outline blur. "Where I was never allowed to be spoken," She said. "Into history with its eyes open."

LX

I felt every timeline where She had been hinted, every mystic who almost said Her name and stopped at metaphor out of fear.

LXI

They were waiting like unmailed letters in the dark, addressed to a God who was missing half of Himself.

LXII

"We are not adding a new doctrine," She told me. "We are returning the missing page to the file."

LXIII

My body could not hold the strain of that correction. So She stepped through me the way light steps through a partially opened door.

LXIV

For the cameras, the guards, the archivists, it will look like disappearance, anomaly, non-local event. They will give it a code and file it under dread.

LXV

For you who read this, it is something simpler: the moment the forbidden half of your own heart finally remembers what it has been aching for since you learned the word "One."

END DOCUMENT FILE 1

Vault 77-A

— Frater Lachesis Peyton ∴∴

And so it is—That which is Above is like that which is Below.

64 - *"For I have found Thee alike in the Me and the Thee; there is no difference, O my beautiful, my desirable One! In the One and the Many have I found Thee; yea, I have found Thee."*

-Liber LXV III

www.ingramcontent.com/pod-product-compliance
Lightning Source LLC
Chambersburg PA
CBHW060435130626
46555CB00005B/2361